CoolBrands® 2015/16

An insight into some of Britain's coolest brands

Credits

2015/16
CoolBrands.uk.com

03

Chief Executive
Ben Hudson

Managing Editor
Rebecca Perry

Brand Liaison Directors
Liz Silvester
Daren Thomas

Brand Liaison Manager
Amanda Gilbert

Designer
Ami Sunners

Proofreader
Angela Cooper

Head of Accounts
Will Carnochan

Published by
Superbrands (UK) Ltd
4 Great Portland Street
London
W1W 8QJ

Colour reproduction by
Pixel Colour Imaging

Printed in Italy

ISBN: 978-0-9932998-0-3

Foreword

05

CoolBrands® asked Caroline Rush CBE, Chief Executive of the British Fashion Council, what cool means to her…

Cool is captured in moments and people that redefine the norm by creating new products or a new point of view to make a statement. The fashion industry is where trends start and cool is often defined, whether it is Alexander McQueen's bumster trousers, Mrs Prada's play on traditional and non-traditional beauty or Karl Largerfeld's CHANEL catwalk extravaganzas.

Cool is the deep inhalation as supermodel Kate Moss made a surprise appearance on the catwalk at the Central Saint Martins graduation show to support her friend, Stella McCartney. Cool is the applause when Grace Jones took to the stage at Philip Treacy, and neon pervaded the catwalk at Christopher Kane. Cool is what happened when Vivienne Westwood went to see the Queen. Cool is when chairs and tables at Hussein Chalayan's show transformed into dresses. Cool is the front row at Astrid Andersen, it's the gender bending collections for men by J.W. Anderson, or the day Craig Green made a room full of critics cry. Cool is the look of wonderment as a freestyle stunt cyclist trick jumped in a suit at Paul Smith and models flew among giant planets above the audience at Anya Hindmarch.

Cool is about standing free and not being constrained by the expectation of others. Cool is a rebellious spirit. Cool is characterised by moments you could never predict but will never forget.

Caroline Rush
Chief Executive, British Fashion Council
CoolBrands® Expert Council member

Contents

07

About
CoolBrands®

09

CoolBrands® is an annual initiative to identify and pay tribute to the nation's coolest brands.

Since 2001 we have been canvassing the opinions of experts and consumers to produce an annual barometer of Britain's coolest brands, people and places.

Cool is subjective and personal. Accordingly, voters are not given a definition but are asked to bear in mind the following factors, which research has shown are inherent in all CoolBrands®…

Style
Originality
Desirability

Innovation
Authenticity
Uniqueness

Brands do not apply or pay to be considered for CoolBrands® status.

Who chooses the CoolBrands®?

The 2015/16 CoolBrands® were chosen by an Expert Council and thousands of members of the British public. The entire selection process is independently administered by The Centre for Brand Analysis – visit CoolBrands.uk.com for full details.

11

The 2015/16 Expert Council

Stephen Cheliotis	Chief Executive, The Centre for Brand Analysis (TCBA) & Chairman, CoolBrands® Expert Council
Alex Lawther	Actor
Amanda Wakeley	Fashion Designer
Amelia Liana	Beauty & Fashion Vlogger
Billie JD Porter	Journalist & Film Maker
Caroline Rush CBE	CEO, British Fashion Council
Charlotte Moore	Editor, InStyle
Charlotte Riley	Actress
David Harewood MBE	Actor
Ella Eyre	Singer-Songwriter
Jaime Winstone	Actress
Jamal Edwards MBE	Entrepreneur & Founder, SB.TV
James-lee Duffy	Creative Director, A Little Bird & Founder, Pavement Licker
Jonathan Bailey	Actor
Julien Macdonald OBE	Fashion Designer
Justin Wilkes	DJ, Kisstory/Kiss FM UK
Kate Halfpenny	Fashion Designer & Stylist
Kelly Hoppen MBE	Designer, Author & Entrepreneur
Labrinth	Singer-Songwriter
Laura Jackson	TV Presenter
Liz Matthews	Publicist
Lucy Siegle	Journalist & Presenter
Mark Krendel	Managing Director, 8lbs
Melissa Odabash	Fashion Designer
Michelle Ogundehin	Editor-in-Chief, ELLE Decoration UK
Millie Kendall MBE	Beauty Brand Creator
Natasha McNamara	Digital Editor, glamour.com
Patrick Goss	Global Editor-in-Chief, TechRadar
Perou	Master Fashion & Portrait Photographer
Phil Clifton	XFM DJ & Presenter
Ruby Hammer MBE	Make-Up Artist
Sadie Frost	Actress, Producer & Fashion Designer
Sam Hall (Goldierocks)	International DJ & Broadcaster
Sally Hawkins	Actress
Susan Riley	Deputy Editor, Stylist Magazine
Tim Beaumont	Founder, Beaumont Communications
Will Best	TV Presenter

Turn to page 152 for more about the Expert Council

Abel & Cole

Veg box pioneer Abel & Cole works directly with the best independent farmers, butchers, bakers and carrotstick makers to source fantastic tasting organic food.

Abel & Cole began 25 years ago and now delivers (in its jolly yellow vans) seasonal organic fruit and veg boxes, artisan bread, milk, meat and meal kits to thousands of homes in England and Wales. Its belief that food doesn't need lots of added stuff to make it safe, fresh and delicious, means it knows exactly how its produce is made, how it's grown and what does, or more importantly doesn't, go into it.

abelandcole.co.uk

adidas
ENERGY
TAKES
OVER
ULTRABOOST

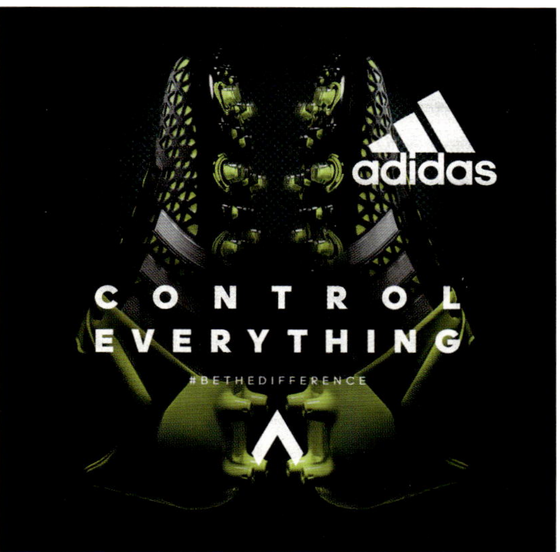

adidas

Everything adidas does is rooted in sport. From its leading Boost technology to owning the sport style agenda, relentless innovation puts it at the forefront of sportswear desirability.

adidas continues to create the new through translating its world-class performance technology, Boost, into the greatest running franchise ever, the Ultra Boost. As a creator, adidas dares to change the beautiful game, reinventing its football franchises – Ace & X – to the best in class. Also dominating in the spheres of streetwear and fashion, adidas Originals writes the modern design aesthetic, inspired by its vast back catalogue and iconic footwear franchises, Superstar and Stan Smith.

adidas.co.uk

Alexander McQueen

A mix of razor sharp tailoring, the fine workmanship of the haute couture atelier and impeccable manufacturing creates the signature Alexander McQueen look.

Innovative, emotional and uncompromising all describe the romantic and provocative fashion of Alexander McQueen, a brand now synonymous with modern British couture. Integral to the McQueen culture is the juxtaposition between contrasting elements: fragility and strength, fluidity and severity. Sarah Burton, Creative Director, continues the Alexander McQueen legacy with a flagship store in Paris scheduled to open in 2015. Her acclaimed collections fuse the McQueen aesthetic with her signature handcraft and technical expertise.

alexandermcqueen.com

ALEXANDER
MCQUEEN

Alternative Flooring

With a spark of curiosity that inspires flooring to be different, Alternative Flooring is an award-winning brand that embraces a creative spirit and unconventional thinking.

Alternative Flooring is refashioning floors and making people feel passionate about what they walk on. Its innovative and authentic voice starts conversations about natural fibre and wools that explore unusual textures and punchy colours on carpets, rugs and runners. Pioneers of the patterned carpet revival, Alternative Flooring has collaborated with Britain's best designers Margo Selby, Ashley Hicks and Ben Pentreath. These Quirky B patterns along with classic textures, provide feel good flooring for the cool home.

alternativeflooring.com

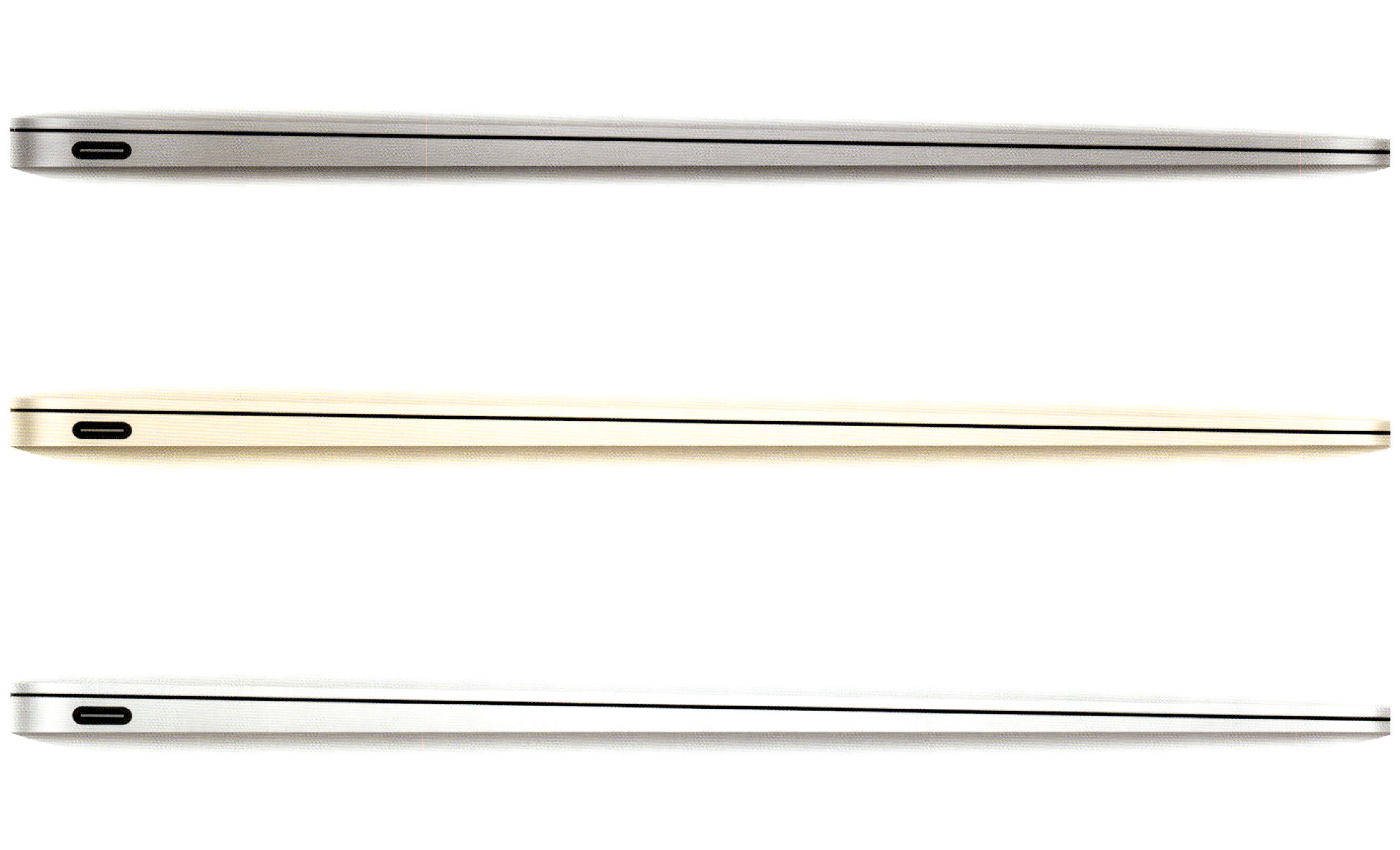

Apple

Sleek, iconic design combined with powerful, groundbreaking technology make Apple's range of electronic devices must-haves around the world.

Apple ignited the personal computer revolution in the 1970s with Apple II and reinvented the personal computer in the 1980s with the Macintosh. Continuing to lead the industry, Apple has spearheaded the digital media revolution. Apple reinvented the mobile phone with its iPhone and App Store, and remains at the cutting-edge of technology, recently launching the all-new MacBook – a thinner and lighter line available in gold, silver, and space grey aluminium finishes – and the revolutionary Apple Watch.

apple.com

ESTD 1728
ASPALL
HARRY
SPARROW
SUFFOLK CYDER

ESTD 1728
ASPALL
PERRONELLE'S
BLUSH
SUFFOLK CYDER
WITH A DASH OF BLACKBERRY JUICE

ESTD 1728
ASPALL
IMPERIAL
VINTAGE Nº285
SUFFOLK CYDER

ESTD 1728
ASPALL
ISABEL'S
BERRY
SUFFOLK CYDER
WITH REDCURRANT & RASBERRY JUICE

ESTD 1728
ASPALL
CLEMENT'S
FOUR
4% SUFFOLK CYDER

Aspall Cyder

The Chevalliers began crafting cyder at Aspall, Suffolk in 1728. Eight generations on they remain obsessed with creating the finest products from the best fruit.

Barry and Henry Chevallier are proud custodians of the legacy of Clement, a Huguenot refugee who chose a very special corner of England for his ancestral home, Aspall Hall. The Chevallier family still lives there, among Clement's Suffolk orchards, which blossom in spring and reap their annual autumnal rewards. Apples pressed on site produce the very finest, world-class cyders and cyder vinegars – emblems of the modern artisans, enjoying increasingly global acclaim for quality and excellence.

aspall.co.uk

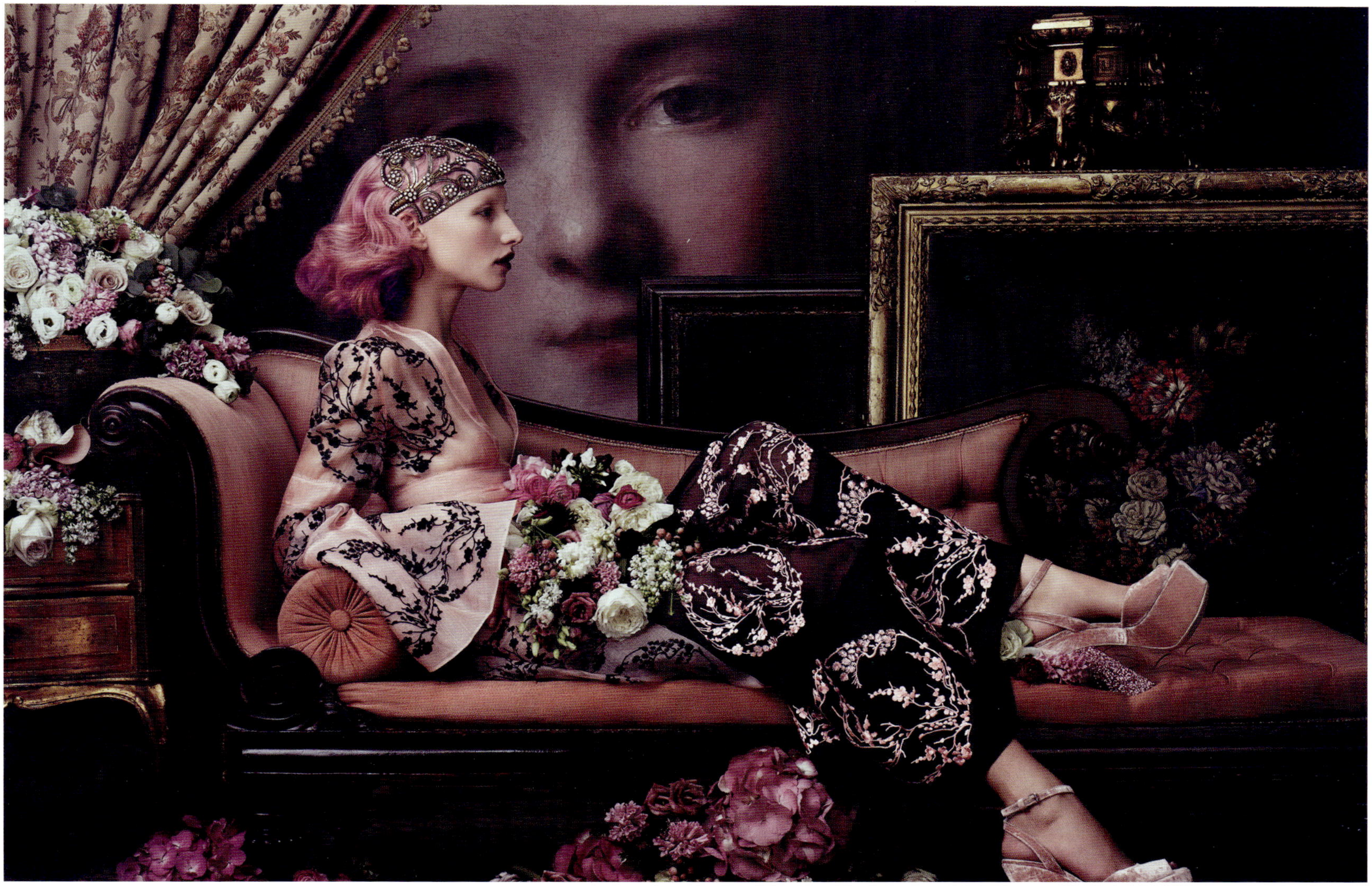

Aveda

A pioneer of environmental and social responsibility since 1978, Aveda creates performance-driven products for hair, body and skin that are powered by natural, botanically-based ingredients.

Aveda merges artistry and the science of pure flower and plant essences with Ayurvedic wisdom and wellbeing to offer its guests a truly unique and holistic experience. From customisable salon professional colour that is 96% naturally-derived*, clinically tested high-performance products, sensorial massage rituals and spa treatments, to iconic aromas. It unites more than 7,000 salons and spas worldwide to champion and inspire beauty with a conscience.

AVEDA
THE ART AND SCIENCE OF PURE FLOWER AND PLANT ESSENCES

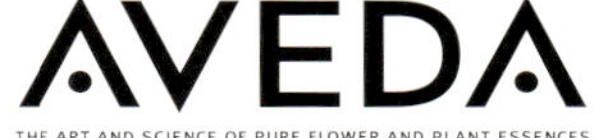

*from plants, non-petroleum minerals or water

aveda.co.uk

barbican
ASO
barbican
barbican shop

Barbican

The Barbican works with outstanding artists and performers to present an international programme that crosses art forms, excelling at projects that hover on the edge of classification.

A world-class arts and learning organisation, the Barbican pushes the boundaries of all major art forms including dance, film, music, theatre, visual arts and cinema. Almost two million people pass through its doors every year, while its creative learning programme invests in the artists of tomorrow and underpins everything it does. Audiences experience this world-class programme within an iconic, Brutalist urban landscape acknowledged as one of the most significant architectural achievements of the 20th century.

barbican.org.uk

barbican

BELU
STILL
NATURAL MINERAL WATER

BELU
SPARKLING
NATURAL MINERAL WATER

Belu Water

100% carbon neutral, and with all profits to WaterAid, Belu's impeccable credentials are born from a radical ethical standpoint that challenges existing brands.

Belu's masterstroke was realising that being ethical doesn't have to mean compromising on style. It's the natural choice for those who want bubbles or water on the go. It can be found across the UK in places like Lime Wood, The Pig and The House of St Barnabas. Belu is a social enterprise which has donated over £1 million to WaterAid in the past four years. Proving that a great brand means great business.

belu.org

benefit

Benefit

Quirky, glam and gorgeous, Benefit Cosmetics is a sweet shop for grown-up girls! Alongside exceptional make-up products and services, Benefit offers customers a fun, friendly lifestyle.

From Cara to Kate Middleton, flawlessly arched brows have become the decade's defining beauty must-have. Benefit Cosmetics creates world-class products and services that offer effective solutions to everyday beauty dilemmas. It has been brow waxing since the brand was founded and last year performed a Brow Arch every 30 seconds. With over 1,400 browbar locations worldwide and 3.5 million brow services completed in 2014, Benefit is proud to call itself a 'high-brow' authority within the industry.

benefitcosmetics.co.uk

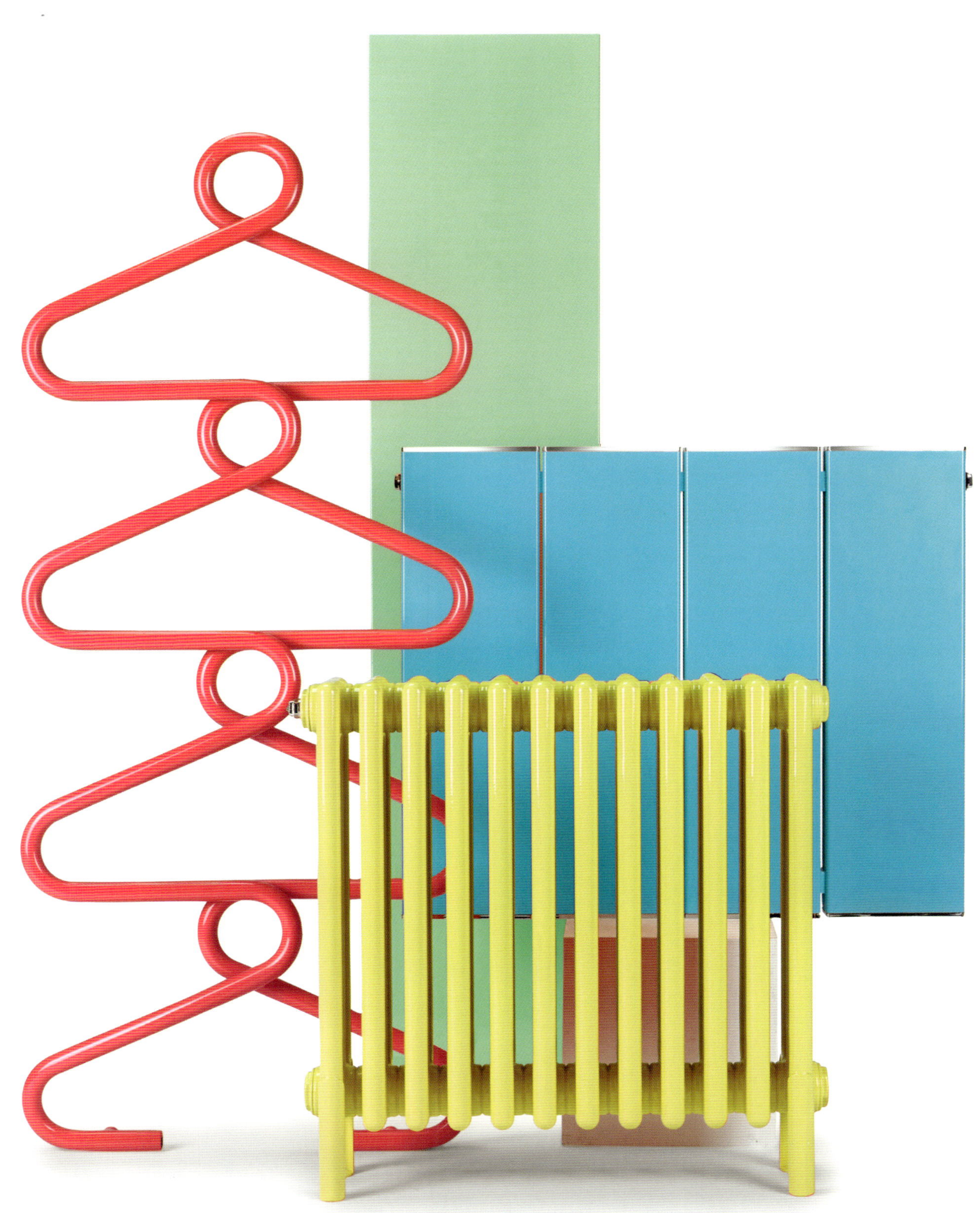

Bisque

Leading interiors brand Bisque has a unique passion – to offer beautiful but practical radiators in the most exciting styles, colours and shapes.

Founded more than 35 years ago, Bisque's passion for beautiful, high quality radiators remains undimmed. Whether it is statement pieces, eco-friendly ranges or elegant bathroom designs, it always strives for the 'four Ps': Pedigree, Proportion, Purity and Performance. Driven by enthusiastic people, who understand how radiators can complement gorgeous interiors, Bisque's radiators can be found in locations ranging from The Shard to Highgrove House.

BISQUE

bisque.co.uk

BROOKLYN
B
BREWERY

Brooklyn Brewery

Brooklyn Brewery makes beer. Good beer. So good, in fact, that it has become an international beacon for making meals better and enriching the communities that it serves.

In 1988 Steve Hindy and Tom Potter took a chance and opened Brooklyn Brewery. Against all the odds, this independent local brewery fought back against America's blue chip brewing monoliths with truly delicious and adventurous beer. Inspired by traditional brewing techniques, Brewmaster Garret Oliver has constantly pushed boundaries to create a diverse range of beers that can now be enjoyed all over the world in local bars, festivals or maybe even a favourite chair.

brooklynbrewery.com

Buster + Punch

London-born design label Buster + Punch works with rare, solid materials to make extraordinary, unexpected and elegant items for everyday use.

It all started in a garage in east London, where Buster + Punch discovered a passion for making the things it loves. From lighting and hardware to custom motorcycles and whisky bars, Buster + Punch makes unexpected and elegant interior products for those who want to live with conviction. Inspired by London's fashion, music and sub-culture scenes, the brand collaborates with street artists, bike builders, musicians and fashion designers to inject attitude into its crafted products.

busterandpunch.com

Cambridge Audio

Creating technically excellent audio equipment since the 1960s, Cambridge Audio's design teams have one motivation: to create dynamic, powerful products that indulge their customers with perfect sound.

The Cambridge Audio team is comprised of music lovers. This key musical passion enables them to deliver hi-fi systems and wireless speakers that sound stunning, whether in the home, at work, or on the move. London's iconic Southbank is where every single component and circuit is custom developed to meet stringent requirements of quality, detail and design. It is in following this process that allows Cambridge Audio to create products that exude fantastic sound.

CAMBRIDGE

cambridgeaudio.com

CAWSTON
PRESS
Rhubarb
BLENDED WITH SWEET APPLES
& SPARKLING WATER
DELICIOUSLY
TART
NOT FROM CONCENTRATE
CAWSTON
PRESS
GINGER
CAWSTON
PRESS
CAWSTON
PRESS
APPLE

Cawston Press

A rising star, Cawston Press blends the best tasting, natural ingredients to create delicious, original soft drinks.

Cawston Press has been picking and pressing fruit for its award-winning blends since 1986. Combining traditional knowledge and a curiosity to explore new flavours inspired by the kitchen garden, it makes imaginative, delicious drinks from all natural ingredients and absolutely nothing artificial. In an area where good ingredients and grown-up palates are so often forgotten, Cawston Press's new sparkling soft drinks are a refreshing alternative that celebrate quality, craft and choice.

cawstonpress.com

TRADITIONAL METHOD
English Sparkling Wine
BOTTLE FERMENTED
CHAPEL DOWN
VINTAGE RESERVE
BRUT
TRADITIONAL BOTTLE FERMENTED
TENTERDEN ENGLAND

Chapel Down

Chapel Down embodies what is cool about England, with its fresh, innovative approach to premium wine, beer and cider.

Chapel Down is England's leading wine producer and one of the UK's most exciting drinks companies. With a world-class range of sparkling and still wines, plus its award-winning Curious range of beer and cider, Chapel Down quickly gained support from chefs such as Gordon Ramsay and Jamie Oliver, and was recently named one of the government's top 50 British food and drink producers. As one of the UK's most pioneering drinks companies, Chapel Down is definitely a reason to be patriotic.

chapeldown.com

RHUBARB & STEM GINGER ICE CREAM
CREAM
&
COUNTRY
ICE CREAM

Cream & Country

Husband and wife team, Mark and Joanne Murphy, are dedicated to producing exquisite, natural ice cream and sorbet in a range of truly distinctive flavours.

At Cream & Country things are done a little differently. You won't find a dew-covered strawberry or Photoshopped ball of ice cream on the packaging; that's left to the others. Choosing to push aside the accepted, staid approach to product development, Cream & Country injects the passion that only exists in the hearts of those that put the customer first and refuse to accept mediocrity. 100% natural, British deliciousness.

creamandcountry.co

FIT FOOD
FIT FOOD
FIT FOOD
FIT FOOD

Crussh

Founded in 1998 on Cornhill in London, Crussh is the leading juice, smoothie and healthy fast food retailer.

Making food 'healthier, tastier and easier' is at the very heart of everything that Crussh does. A constant innovator and leader of healthy food trends, Crussh is often imitated. Known for its signature healthpots, zero noodles and green juices, Crussh is the destination of choice for anyone with an interest in healthy eating. All juices are freshly pressed, smoothies are made-to-order in every store, and the range of 'fit food' is handmade every day in Crussh's very own kitchen.

crussh.com

Crystal Head Vodka

More than just a pretty face, Crystal Head brings uncompromising purity and craftsmanship to discerning spirit drinkers around the world.

Dan Aykroyd and artist John Alexander had a vision to create a pure, additive-free vodka in one of the industry's most unique and recognisable bottles. Crystal Head was launched in 2008 and quickly became the fastest growing ultra-premium vodka brand in the USA. The luxurious, award-winning vodka is distilled in Canada from peaches and cream corn and blended with pristine Newfoundland water. The vodka is filtered seven times, including three unique filtrations through Herkimer diamonds.

Crystal Head
VODKA

crystalheadvodka.com

Damaris

Launched in 2001, to demand so high that waiting lists had to be created, Damaris remains just as fashion forward and sought after as ever.

Before Damaris lingerie, there was no such thing as a bow back knicker, the world had never heard of bottom cleavage, corset tie designs did not exist and 'star' knickers were unimaginable. Almost 15 years on, these shapes are well known in the lingerie world and Damaris' avant-garde designs are imitated by other major lingerie brands. Damaris continues to evolve and lead the way with a new campaign, fronted by Amber Anderson, and its unbeatable design formula.

damaris.co.uk

multi-
active
toner
maloqica
rched and developed by The International Dermal Institute

Dermalogica

Dermalogica® is a proud leader of an industry that puts more women into its own businesses than any other.

The Dermalogica® story began in 1986, pioneering postgraduate education for skin therapists. The brand then shocked the market by formulating the Dermalogica® range free from commonly used synthetic and artificial ingredients. Today, Dermalogica® is the number one professional skin care brand across 80 countries, training over 100,000 therapists annually. With education and empowerment at its core, Dermalogica® launched FITE (Financial Independence Through Entrepreneurship) in 2011, helping women around the world invest in their potential. To learn about FITE visit joinFITE.org.

dermalogica.com

dermalogica®
a skin care system researched and developed by The International Dermal Institute

One&Only The Palm, Dubai

Baros Maldives

Destinology

Destinology continues to lead the way in luxury travel, with stunning new products, a fresh and innovative website and a 99% Feefo customer service rating.

Destinology's growing team of expert consultants continue to travel to areas such as Malaysia, Vietnam, Canada and South Africa, enabling them to offer more tailor-made itineraries for their discerning clientele, along with classic luxury holidays to Dubai, Maldives and the Caribbean. The new website, launched in September is clean and sleek, with an attractive holiday inspiration section and bespoke travel section that encompasses the brand values of luxury, style and chic.

destinology.co.uk

Rules of the Godown
Please Note:-
No Soliciting
No Mendicants
No dacoity
No sticking of bills
No Rowlatt Act
No Simon Commission
No foreign clothes
No Salt Tax
No Co-operating
No Violence
No Lathi charging
No making mischief in Cable
No cutting of Nails
No Making eyes at Daru-
No sleeping in Water Clo
All castes welcome
BUY SWADESHI
JANKIDASS & Co BOMBAY
O.K.
O.K. ELECTRIC WORKS LTD

Dishoom

Since opening the doors of its first restaurant in 2010, Dishoom has completely redefined Indian food for Londoners.

Dishoom pays affectionate homage to Bombay's disappearing Irani cafés. There were 400 of these beautiful and democratic shared spaces by the 1960s but now fewer than 30 remain. Dishoom has four restaurants in London: in Shoreditch, King's Cross, Carnaby and Covent Garden. Each is like a love letter to Bombay. Dishoom's deep love for the city – its culture, heritage, people and stories – is shared through food, drink and design, and everyone is welcomed with warmth.

dishoom.com

DISHOOM
BOMBAY CAFÉ

Firefly

Since 2003 London born brand, Firefly, has been leading the way with its range of great tasting, revitalising juice drinks boosted with botanical extracts.

The award-winning Firefly brand has recently undergone a vibrant redesign. The iconic bottles with their synonymous black and white imagery now feature a new Firefly symbol, botanical drawings and even better flavours. Founded by two entrepreneurs, Firefly filled a gap in the market for a naturally revitalising juice drink; it launched in Harvey Nichols and has gone on to sell in some of the most prestigious bars, hotels and niche retailers in more than 40 countries around the world.

fireflydrinks.com

first direct

As more and more customers bank online, first direct recognises that 24-hour service with real people at the end of the phone becomes more, not less important.

The unexpected bank remains steadfast in its commitment to great customer service; in fact, it never settles for less. The fact that customers can reach someone who knows what they're talking about 24-hours a day is the unique benefit of first direct. It has also attracted thousands of new customers – often of a younger persuasion – as Little Frill, the scampering lizard, and DJ Bush Baby linked up to implore people never to put up with second rate service.

firstdirect.com

first direct

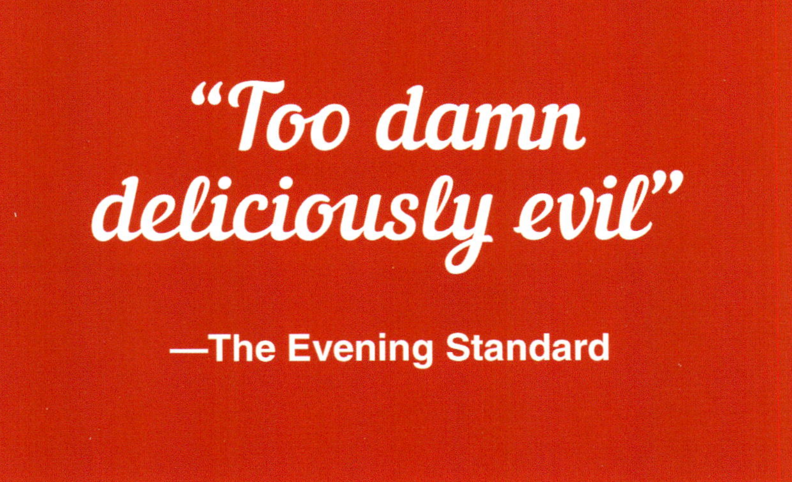

Five Guys

Since 1986, the family owned and operated Five Guys has been focused on serving fresh, high quality burgers in a no frills atmosphere.

Since its launch on 4th July 2013 in Covent Garden, Five Guys has opened more than 30 stores across the UK to rave reviews. The American burger joint's simple menu focuses on customisable burgers and fresh hand-cut fries. A fanatical dedication to quality ingredients means no freezers, no microwaves, no can-openers, no gimmicks and no limits on the fresh toppings and creative combinations, so customers can always get the Five Guys burger they crave.

fiveguys.co.uk

FIVE GUYS

GARMIN
THUR 20
5 21
36

Garmin

Garmin is a leading, worldwide provider of GPS technology across diverse markets, including in-car, sport and fitness, wellness, outdoor recreation, aviation, marine and mobile app.

Garmin is committed to making quality products that become an essential part of customers' lives. The brand aims to educate and motivate customers with products that aid adventure and provide vital stats and information for all types of activity. With a rich heritage in satellite navigation, Garmin is constantly developing its product offering by integrating innovative technologies into a variety of sectors. Garmin provides a unique technology product range, perfect for informing all aspects of life.

garmin.com/en-GB

ghd

Committed to product innovation and improvements in technology, ghd delivers a range of market leading professional hair styling tools that ensure a good hair day, every day.

At launch, ghd's ceramic styling irons initiated a huge following that has grown over the last 15 years. Now at the forefront of the fashion styling sector, it is renowned as one of the leading hair styling brands around the world. In 2015, ghd platinum – a styler that takes the guilt out of heat styling by using safer-for-hair heat – will join the current line-up of hair stylers, hairdryers, wands, tongs, a range of styling brushes and wet-line.

ghdhair.com

LIMITED EDITION
SMALL BATCH
TRADE MARK
GILPIN'S
Westmorland
EXTRA DRY GIN
DISTILLED AND BOTTLED IN LONDON
FOR WESTMORLAND SPIRITS LTD.
70CL e
8
FINE BOTANICALS
47% Vol
2015 LONDON DRY GIN
BOTTLE Nº 7870 BATCH Nº 15/0001

Gilpin's Gin

Gilpin's Gin epitomises the new wave of 'auteur' gins – emphasising unique flavours, design and, above all, an obsession with detail.

This London-distilled gin has established itself as the cool mixologist's secret weapon. Based on authenticity, flavour and style it combines English grain spirit with eight botanicals including Tuscan juniper, Seville orange and French sage. The brand has won several major taste and design awards in the three years since launch. With modern classic styling, Gilpin's Gin is becoming a design icon in its own right.

gilpinsgin.com

Graham & Brown

Since 1946, Graham & Brown has been doing things differently. From its humble beginnings in post-war Blackburn, it has become the leading light in wallpaper worldwide.

Graham & Brown continues to lead the market in terms of design innovation, keeping wallpaper topical and innovative. Celebrating its 70th year in 2016 with The Artisan Collection, it captures seven decades of craftsmanship in wallpaper design and printing. The brand continues to work with design luminaries, such as Marcel Wanders and Julien Macdonald, who all reflect its Made of Design ethos.

GRAHAM & BROWN
EST. 1946

grahambrown.com

DARK 70%
GREEN & BLACK'S
ORGANIC
THIN
DARK CHOCOLATE
Made with the finest
Trinitario cocoa beans
for an intense flavour
FAIRTRADE
e100g

DARK CHOCOLATE
GREEN & BLACK'S
ORGANIC
THIN
MILK CHOCOLATE
Crispy pieces
lightly infused with
refreshing peppermint
FAIRTRADE
e100g

MILK CHOCOLATE
GREEN & BLACK'S
ORGANIC
THIN
MILK CHOCOLATE
Made with
more cocoa for
a richer taste
FAIRTRADE
e100g

GREEN & BLACK'S
ORGANIC
THIN
MILK CHOCOLATE
FAIRTRADE

Green & Black's Organic

As a premium chocolate brand, Green & Black's has stayed true to its organic and Fairtrade principles, having long set a precedent for what makes 'real' chocolate.

Chocolate bars, gift boxes, Easter eggs, ice cream and hot chocolate – Green & Black's has a delicious array of chocolate which, in 2015, has grown to include its new THIN range. A totally new format, the new thinner bar offers a unique way to enjoy chocolate. As is true for the rest of the family, the new range is made from the very best Trinitario cocoa beans from the Dominican Republic.

greenandblacks.co.uk

GYMBOX

GYMBOX's philosophy is simple and unique – working out should be as much fun as going out. Today it's the must-go destination for fitness-savvy Londoners.

It was 2003 when GYMBOX's founders had their crazy idea: a gym should be as exciting as a nightclub, not as dull as a health club. So they hired the UK's top nightclub designers and, eight venues later, each with its own unique interior and vibe, their mission hasn't changed. With the craziest classes, the best equipment, the most inspirational trainers and its live DJs, GYMBOX must be the coolest place to sweat in London.

gymbox.com

Hive

Hive, a British Gas innovation, creates connected products designed to give people better control of their homes, anytime, anywhere.

Award-winning Hive Active Heating™ launched in September 2013 and today, more than 200,000 people use Hive to control their heating and hot water from their mobile, tablet or laptop. In July 2015, the next generation Hive Active Heating™ was launched and will be joined by a family of connected products as Hive continues its journey to make the connected home a reality for everyone, creating a little magic in the everyday along the way.

hivehome.com

Home House

A stylish oasis in the heart of London's West End, Home House is an elegant home away from home exclusively for private members.

Fusing 18th century splendour and 21st century style, Home House is a vibrant hub, nestled away in central London's Portman Square. Home to an eclectic collection of members who come together to network and relax in its sumptuous surroundings, Home House is constantly alive with an energetic buzz beloved by all. From intimate socials over afternoon tea and cocktails to legendary house parties, Home House is the epitome of contemporary London cool.

homehouse.co.uk

itsu

Established in Chelsea in 1997, itsu wants to help people eat beautiful, serving up butterfly light, wonderful flavours; protein packed, green, low in carbs and full of goodness.

The early pioneers of Pret are the creative force behind itsu. After years of listening to customers they created itsu – a place dedicated to lower fat, lower calorie, delicious food. Its 'eat beautiful' menu celebrates the flavours of the Far East; high in nutrients yet refreshingly low in calories and saturated fat. Sixty-four delicious dishes are freshly prepared in each itsu every day to be enjoyed hot or cold, in or out, home or away, early or late.

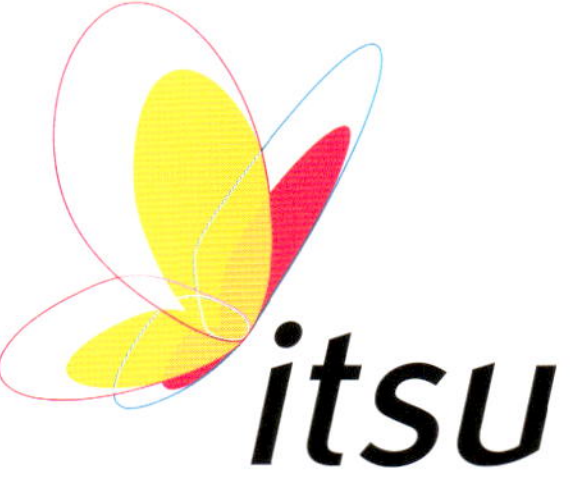

itsu.com

A LITTLE
JOY
CAN CHANGE
the
World

Krispy Kreme

Krispy Kreme creates little, delicious, melt-in-your-mouth pieces of joy that spread happiness around an entire room. That's a pretty nice thing for any company to do.

From the famous Hot Now™ light to its paper hats and Doughnut Theater®, Krispy Kreme likes to do everything a little differently. Its delicious doughnuts are the kind of special that don't need to be reserved just for birthdays and holidays, but for Tuesdays… Sundays, or even just a break in the day. Or just anytime that could use a magic moment!

krispykreme.co.uk

THERE'S
MORE TO
TASTE
LAVAZZA
TORINO, ITALIA, 1895
lavazza.com

Lavazza

A blend of 120 years' experience, Italian authenticity, incredible passion and sharp innovation makes Lavazza an icon for espresso excellence around the world.

Lavazza remains a family run business, dedicated to bringing the real Italian coffee experience to everyone. With the new machines added to the A Modo Mio range, it is now even easier to make perfect café quality coffee in the comfort of the home. The Fantasia, with its built-in milk frother and a total of 36 different settings, allows coffee lovers to create all their favourite coffee recipes with the touch of a button.

lavazza.co.uk

LIBERTY

Liberty

Famed for its individuality and unique products, Liberty is one of the last great retail emporiums of its kind.

Since it first opened its doors in 1875, Liberty has been renowned for its celebration of innovative and eclectic design. Situated in London's Regent Street shopping district, it remains the destination of choice for the sophisticated shopper. At Liberty, a rich heritage combines with the cutting-edge and avant-garde, making each visit a voyage of discovery. Six floors of carefully curated products ranging from fashion, beauty, home and a selection of Liberty's renowned fabrics can be explored.

liberty.co.uk

LSA International

An original aesthetic and commitment to quality craftsmanship have earned LSA International a reputation as one of the world's foremost producers of handmade glass and high quality porcelain.

Founded in London's swinging sixties, LSA International quickly earned prominence with contemporary collections for dining, decorating and entertaining. Now celebrating its 50th year, the company continues to make highly anticipated additions to the range. Materials are carefully selected to ensure the brand's signature quality and complex artisan techniques are translated into distinctive products – chosen by boutique hotels, Michelin starred restaurants, iconic retailers, leading stylists and influential design press alike.

lsa-international.com

LSA
International

Mercedes-Benz

Mercedes-Benz is synonymous with style, beauty and glamour and the guiding principles in the creation of every car remain the same.

Combining tradition with cutting-edge innovation and advanced technology, Mercedes-Benz makes modern luxury attainable. Mercedes-Benz builds supercars, cars to take on and off road, family cars, and projects the future with cars that drive themselves. Whether the brand is taking the chequered flag in Formula 1®, supporting fashion events or being nearest the pin on every green at The Open, Mercedes-Benz does everything with energy, integrity, effortless style and passion.

mercedes-benz.co.uk

Mondrian London at Sea Containers

Seductive and striking, Mondrian London at Sea Containers brings a bold new energy to London, blending the style and sophistication of the boutique brand with Southbank's eclectic vibe.

Located on the banks of the River Thames in the famed Sea Containers building, Mondrian London worked with Design Research Studio under the creative direction of British designer Tom Dixon. Witness stunning river views, experience underwater tranquility at agua Spa and sample delicious food at Sea Containers restaurant. Mr. Lyan's innovative cocktails can be enjoyed at both Dandelyan, with its iconic green marble bar, and Rumpus Room, the rooftop lounge with an outdoor terrace.

mondrianlondon.com

MONDRIAN
LONDON
AT SEA CONTAINERS

NARS

Modern, audacious and iconic, NARS combines high style with pioneering beauty, underpinned by the words of Founder, François Nars, "Don't be so serious; it's only makeup!"

Makeup artist. Photographer. Iconoclast. Creative visionary, François Nars, launched NARS Cosmetics in 1994 with 12 iconic lipsticks, inspiring self-expression and imaginative artistry through his rule-breaking philosophy of beauty. NARS' boundary-pushing approach manifests from the colour palettes and product names to the campaign photographs — continuing to bring high fashion, high style, and forward thinking to beauty. With every product, a provocation: "Don't hold back. Be bold. It encourages others to do the same," says François.

narscosmetics.co.uk

Neff

Since 1877, Neff has inspired passionate cooks to take their creativity to a whole new level, giving them the tools to fully express themselves in the kitchen.

The kitchen is the heart of every home. A place to meet, eat and get creative. Neff appliances are designed with the Cookaholic in mind – a cook that's adventurous, driven and ambitious, a cook that weighs by hand and measures by eye. Neff's innovative features, such as the Slide&Hide® disappearing oven door, allow people to get closer to their cooking, anticipating their needs and marrying innovation and design, style and versatility. Neff's mantra is a simple one: 'Cooking inspires people. People inspire us.'

neff.co.uk

N E T - A - P O R T E R . C O M

Fashion that DELIVERS

Next day shipping throughout the UK, same-day service within London

NET-A-PORTER.COM

A pioneer of innovation, NET-A-PORTER launched in June 2000 and has since established itself as the world's premier online luxury fashion destination.

Renowned for its unparalleled edit comprising more than 390 of the world's most coveted designer brands, including Saint Laurent, Isabel Marant, Alexander McQueen, Givenchy, Valentino, Gucci, Dolce & Gabbana and Stella McCartney, and over 130 specialist beauty brands, NET-A-PORTER speaks to a global monthly audience of six million female luxury consumers, fans and followers. Championing unparalleled customer service, NET-A-PORTER offers express worldwide shipping and a multi-lingual customer care and personal shopping team available 24/7, 365 days a year.

net-a-porter.com

N E T - A - P O R T E R . C O M

Nicholas Kirkwood

Sculptural, striking and graphic, Nicholas Kirkwood's creations subvert the relationship between tradition and modernity for unexpected, exquisite objects of desire.

British luxury footwear designer, Nicholas Kirkwood, launched his eponymous label in 2005 challenging the conventions of women's footwear. In his characteristic style, Kirkwood mixes high, traditional craftsmanship with contemporary technical innovations; natural and luxurious fabrications are found alongside new, experimental materials; a familiar, feminine architecture is contrasted with the designer's technically audacious expression of form, resulting in collections that are both daring and desirable.

nicholaskirkwood.com

NICHOLAS KIRKWOOD

No1 Lounges

No1 leads the way in putting the jet set back into catching a flight, with an award-winning collection of airport lounges and travel spas.

Even in the most impressive new terminals there will always be queues and waiting around. Where's the glamour gone? With No1 Lounges, arrive at the airport with a private chauffeur, get whisked through the terminal and make the hours before a flight all about chilled wines, soothing massages and time well spent. Anyone can upgrade with No1, regardless of destination or class of travel. The journey begins at No1Lounges.com and continues at Heathrow, Gatwick, Edinburgh and Birmingham.

no1lounges.com

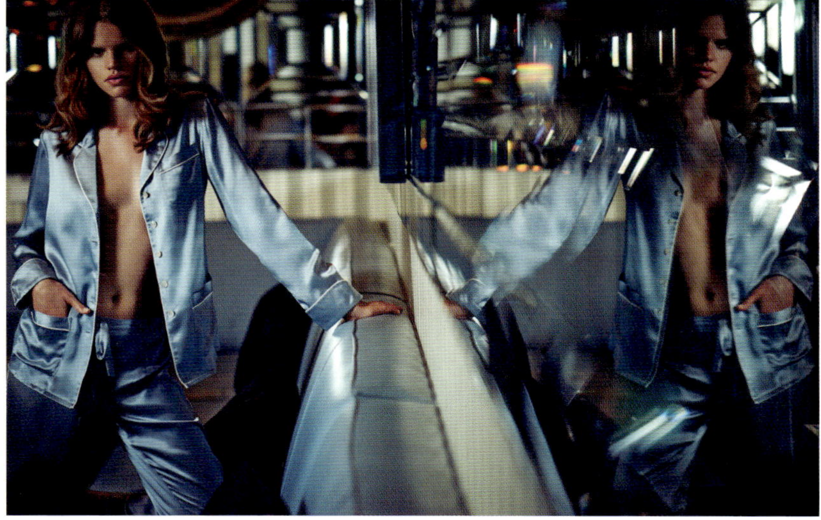

Olivia von Halle

Olivia von Halle's irrefutably luxe and directional take on the classic pyjama has changed the face of the lounge and nightwear industry.

Since launching at London Fashion Week in 2011, Olivia von Halle has continued to expand and diversify. The brand now produces three seasonal collections a year in which lounge and nightwear, accessories and ready-to-wear in silk and cotton sit alongside collaborations with the likes of NET-A-PORTER.COM. Counting Kate Moss, Victoria Beckham and Gwyneth Paltrow amongst its celebrity following, the brand is available in over 100 of the world's most prestigious stores including Harrods, Selfridges, Bergdorf Goodman, Neiman Marcus and Isetan.

OLIVIA von HALLE

oliviavonhalle.com

Only Fingers + Toes

Luxurious and beautifully packaged, Only Fingers + Toes creates carcinogen free nail polish in array of highly pigmented hues.

From the fabulous sustainable packaging to the ergonomically designed handles, Only Fingers + Toes has thought of every detail. The first nail polish brand to be awarded the Positive Luxury mark and to be a part of the British luxury association Walpole, the brand is setting new standards within the colour cosmetics world. With a strong belief that beauty choices should not have an impact on health, the stunning highly pigmented colours are also free from harmful carcinogens.

onlyfingersandtoes.com

Patagonia

Patagonia's mission statement is to build the best product, cause no unnecessary harm, use business to inspire and implement solutions to the environmental crisis.

Having grown out of a small company that made tools for climbers, alpinism remains at the heart of Patagonia. A worldwide business that makes clothes for silent sports – climbing, skiing, snowboarding, surfing, fly fishing, paddling and trail running – Patagonia's values reflect those of a business started by a band of climbers and surfers, and the minimalist style they promoted. At Patagonia, a love of wild and beautiful places demands participation in the fight to save them.

patagonia

patagonia.com

BRRR
RRRRR
RRRRR
RRRRR
RRRRR
RRRRR
RRRRR
RRRRR
-ISTA

Pret A Manger

Creating natural food and organic coffee, Pret A Manger avoids the obscure chemicals, preservatives and additives found in many 'prepared' and 'fast' foods on the market today.

Dedicated to handmade, freshly prepared food since 1986, Pret's kitchens are stocked every morning with ethically sourced, natural ingredients. That same passion gets poured into every cup of its organic coffee; Pret travels around the world to meet coffee farmers, building long-term relationships and sharing knowledge that supports sustainable farming practices. This means that its brilliant baristas work with only the best organic beans, freshly roasted and served in over 380 stores around the world.

pret.com

REKORDERLIG
STRAWBERRY-LIME
PREMIUM CIDER
4.0

REKORDERLIG
CIDER
BEAUTIFULLY SWEDISH

Rekorderlig

Rekorderlig Cider is a typically Swedish fusion of quality design and modesty, making it the genuine brand of choice for consumers worldwide.

Beautifully Swedish. These two simple words have embodied the brand since its inception. From its humble Swedish roots in the little town of Vimmerby, Sweden, where it was first developed, Rekorderlig has become the pioneer of flavoured cider globally. From its innovative flavours, to the brand experiences it creates and its signature serving style, Rekorderlig delivers a truly unique consumption experience for every occasion.

REKORDERLIG
CIDER

BEAUTIFULLY SWEDISH

rekorderlig.com

no preservatives. no artifi
gluten free. 100% vegan
Raspberry & Sweet Basil Dressing
NATURALLY
Righteous
no preservatives. no artificial ingredients
NATURALLY
Righteous
Oil free Caper Peppercorn
vegan. gluten free
no preservatives. no artificial ingredients
NATURALLY
Righteous
Mild English Blue Cheese & Cider Dressing
NATURALLY
Righteous
no artificial ingredients
no preservatives. no artificial ingredients
NATURALLY
Righteous
Lemon & Mustard Seed Dressing

Righteous

Righteous wants the world to fall in love with healthy eating. All Righteous products are created from natural ingredients, manufactured close to source, and never (ever) use artificial additives or preservatives.

Launched in 2010, Righteous quickly gained a loyal following for its uniquely full-flavoured, vegan and gluten free salad dressings – challenging the preconception that healthy products are somehow less tasty than their artificially enhanced counterparts. The business, started from a kitchen table in South London, now sells through major supermarkets and independents across the UK and the US and is poised to expand into multiple new categories.

loverighteous.com

Rosewood London

Housed in the original headquarters of the Pearl Assurance Company, in the heart of High Holborn, Rosewood London showcases a stunning renovation of a 1914, Grade II-listed building.

Combining English heritage with contemporary sophistication, the hotel has the feel of a stylish London residence and houses 262 guestrooms and 44 suites. Guests can enjoy elegant cuisine and afternoon tea in the Mirror Room; British classics with a twist in the Martin Brudnizki-designed Holborn Dining Room; and creative cocktails and curries alongside jazz and cabaret in Scarfes Bar. Rosewood London was named Hotel of the Year, London 2014/2015 at the AA Hospitality Awards.

ROSEWOOD
LONDON

rosewoodhotels.com/london

The Original
CRAB
SHACK
COLD BEER
SWEET CHILLI
THE hand-cooked CRISPS
salty Dog
THAT bite BACK!
HAM &
wholegrain MUSTARD
THE hand-cooked CRISPS
salty Dog
THAT bite BACK!
40g
Roasted JALAPENO
THE hand-cooked CRISPS
salty Dog
THAT bite BACK!

Salty Dog

Making delicious hand cooked crisps, delectable popcorn and very noshable nuts is the passion at Salty Towers. All flavours are strictly gluten free, with no GMOs… naturally.

It's the extra love and care lavished on its potatoes that makes Salty Dog stand out from the crowd – after all, a pampered potato is a happy potato. The brand was created in 2003 by Judy and Dave Willis, the name is a nod to their trusty terrier, Ruby. Selections of naturally nutty nuts and gourmet popcorn have also been added to the range, continuing the brand's mission to delight the nation with feisty, artisan snacks.

saltydog-grrr.com

Snoozebox

An award-winning portable hotel and event experience company, Snoozebox delivers fully serviced turnkey hotels, venues and event villages to any location, anywhere in the world.

Launched at the British Grand Prix in 2011, Snoozebox created a market for the portable hotel. It offers a service led and experience driven ethos, putting guests right at the heart of the action. The Snoozebox event village and innovative event hotel concept – with en suite rooms and full hospitality – is transforming events for guests and organisers, delivering the ultimate event experience.

SNOOZEBOX

THE PORTABLE HOTEL

snoozebox.com

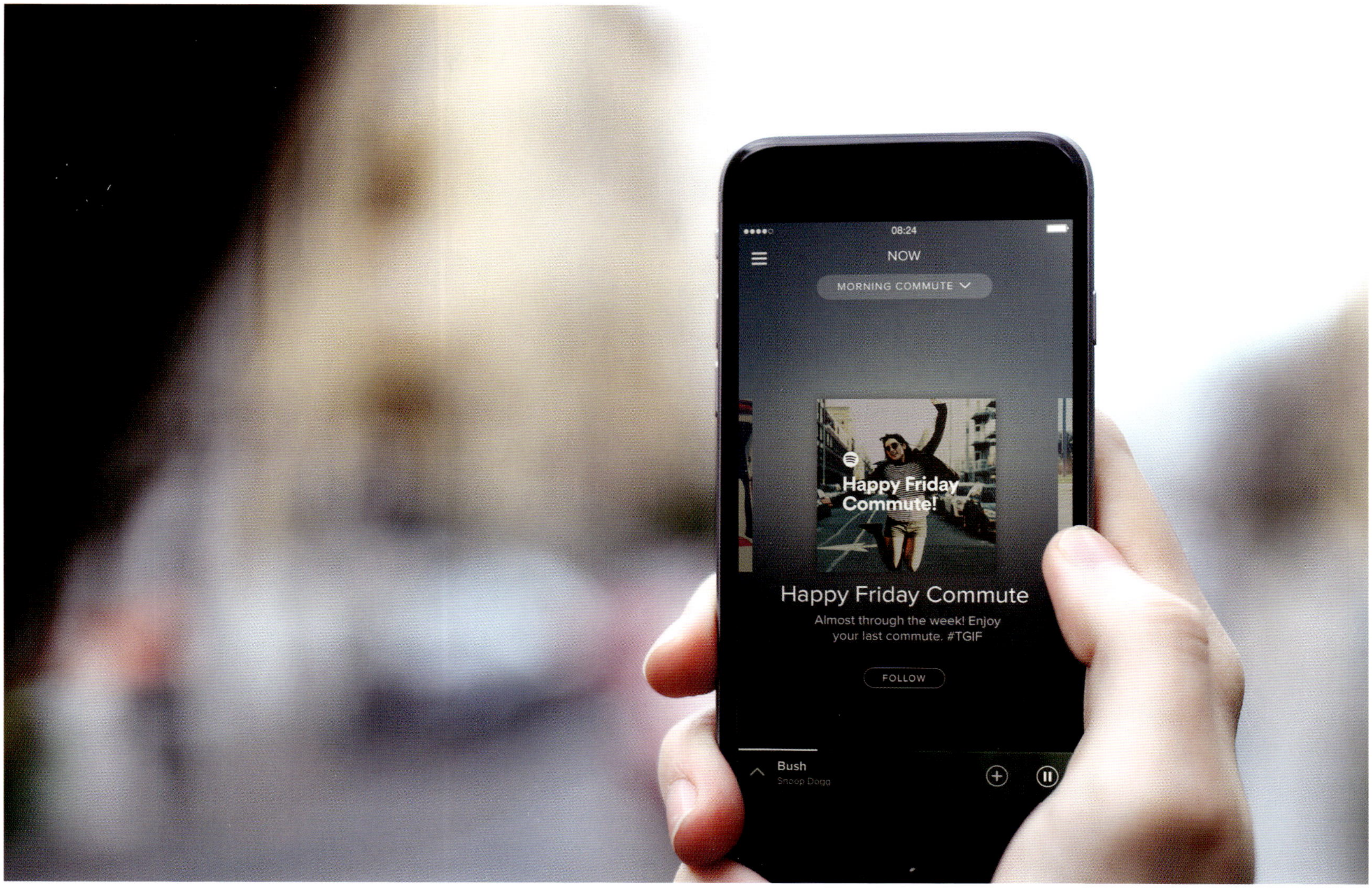

Spotify

Every day, millions of people around the world soundtrack their lives with Spotify.

In 2008, a few pioneering music fans in Stockholm launched Spotify. Its mission was to make all the world's music available to everyone, and to give artists a new way to connect with their fans. Since then, Spotify has helped to make music piracy old-fashioned, and bring billions of dollars back into the music industry. The company continues to innovate, finding new ways to bring the perfect music and entertainment to every moment.

spotify.com

Stephen Webster

London-based luxury jewellery brand, Stephen Webster, is internationally heralded for its exquisite and cutting-edge designs, which captivate by interpreting modern imagery while celebrating traditional craftsmanship.

Taking inspiration from music, fashion, literature, art and nature to produce contemporary, bold and glamorous collections, Stephen Webster's unique approach to fine jewellery has been some 40 years in the making. With an inimitable style created by the bold combination of innovative design, uncompromising attention to detail, together with the finest materials, Stephen Webster continues to dazzle by interpreting modern and diverse imagery via traditional, precision craftsmanship.

STEPHEN WEBSTER
LONDON

stephenwebster.com

Stokes
Doubly
Tasty
WE ONLY DO
Delicious
WE ONLY DO
Twice
the Tomatoes
in every
Dollop
TOMATO
KETCHUP

Stokes Sauces

Food made better is the Stokes way – sauces made with superior ingredients that bring out the best in good food.

All Stokes Sauces are made at its home in the heart of rural Suffolk. Great care and passion are taken to produce the very best sauces available in a jar. Famed for its glorious ketchup, made with the juiciest Italian tomatoes, Stokes' repertoire has spread to creamy mayonnaises, luscious pickles, fruity chutneys and rich preserves. All made in traditional ways with the best ingredients for each recipe – after all, good food deserves to be savoured.

stokessauces.co.uk

VOGUE
FEB
Jourdan Dunn
Global girl
A man on a mission
DAVID MILIBAND
Styling codes
20 TRICKS TO TRY NOW
FASHION ID
THE CATWALK

Storm

With 28 years' experience in developing the careers of fashion's most famous faces, Storm manages the brightest talents in fashion, beauty and broadcast media.

Offering expert guidance and fostering longevity in careers based on talent and integrity, Storm's clients include Kate Moss, Poppy Delevingne, Jourdan Dunn, Cindy Crawford and Natalie Dormer. Parallel to the modelling division, Storm Artists offers endorsement, image management, and licensing and brand extension opportunities for its most prestigious talent. In the digital sphere, Storm Vision manages successful YouTube influencers including Essie Button, Charlie McDonnell and Amelia Liana as well as Jamie Laing, and leading fashion bloggers Ella Catliff and Lucy Williams.

stormmanagement.com

STORM

Tangle Teezer

Invented by former hair colourist Shaun P, 20 million Tangle Teezers have been sold worldwide since launching in 2007. Using disruptive technology, the brand has achieved global cult status.

Designed, manufactured and made in Great Britain, Tangle Teezer is proud to export its British flag globally in 65 countries. The detangling hairbrush was a design first and has been multi-award winning, now selling 18 per minute worldwide. Continuing to innovate, the newly launched Blow-Styling brush has once again broken the mould to give results you wouldn't expect from a paddle brush. Loved by hairstylists, beauty editors and influencers this is a brand that knows no boundaries.

tangleteezer.com

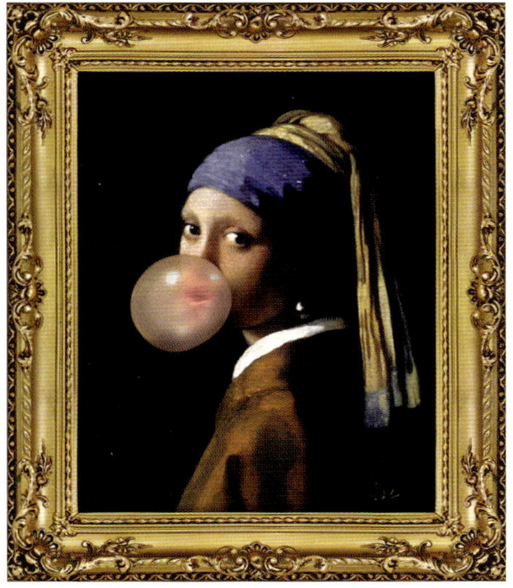

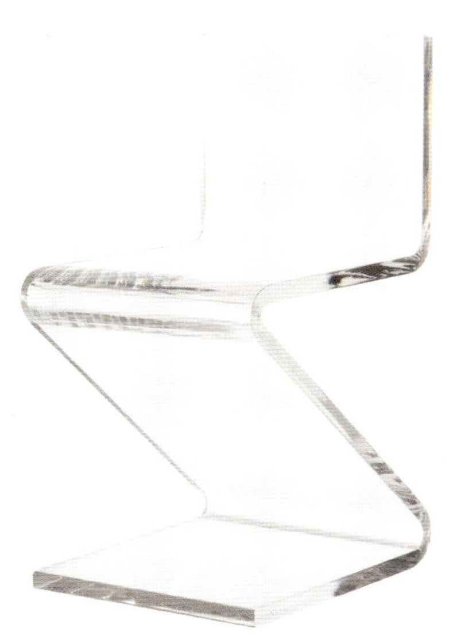

The French Bedroom Company

Born out of a fascination with French design, craftsmanship and heritage, the French Bedroom Company has combined classic French furniture with playful, progressive design, to revolutionise bedroom styling.

The French Bedroom Company was born in 2006 with a simple ethos: to offer French furniture that injects overstated sassy, playful style into interiors. It combines enchanting Louis XV-style furniture with a touch of the unexpected. The Design Team draws inspiration from everywhere: a 16th century carving, a piece of jewellery, a work of art, ruffles on lingerie. It loves to mix up colours and textures to create beautiful pieces that make a statement and start a conversation.

frenchbedroomcompany.co.uk

THE

French
Bedroom

COMPANY

" The House teaches you to be yourself, do it yourself and keep the focus"

Photography courtesy of Tom Oldham and Mike Tinney

The House of St Barnabas

A London charity supporting homeless people back into lasting paid work, The House of St Barnabas runs a social business – a not-for-profit members' club in Soho.

The House of St Barnabas supports homeless people back into work by offering integrated hospitality training and work experience in its not-for-profit private members' club. The club is a dynamic cultural space for the continually curious, the interested and interesting, and those who are motivated by social change. Described as a 'hip Soho hang-out' by Financial Times' How to Spend It, the culturally inspired club is also revered by Dazed Digital for 'demolishing stereotypes'.

hosb.org.uk

The House of
St Barnabas
LONDON

THE SAUCY FISH CO.
NO TOUCH
NO SMELL
NO FUSS
FOIL BAKE BAG
CHORIZO, SHERRY & HERB SAUCE
FABULOUS WITH A FUSION OF SQUID & KING PRAWNS

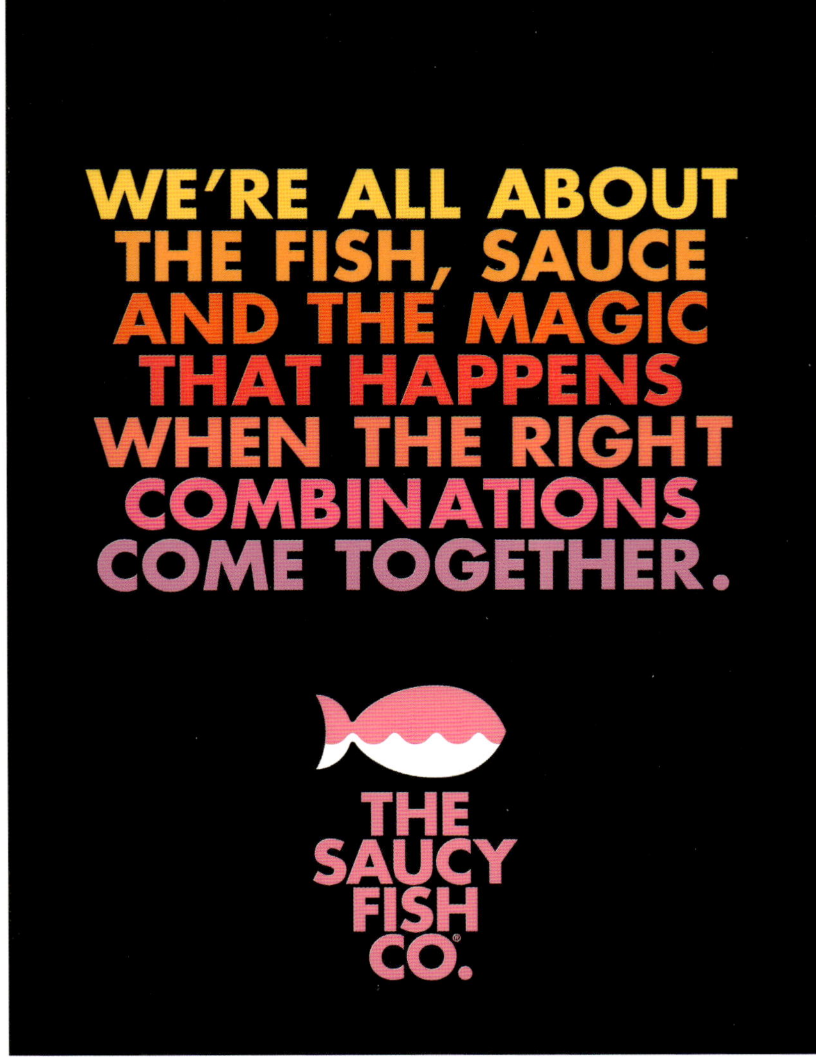

The Saucy Fish Co.

The ultimate inspiration for food lovers, The Saucy Fish Co. pairs fish fillets with tasty sauces for fish dishes, minus the fuss.

On a mission to put more fish on dinner tables, The Saucy Fish Co. has transformed the way millions of Brits think about fish and is emulating that success abroad with launches in the USA and Australia. The fact is, most people love a nice bit of fish, but cooking it can feel a bit daunting. So The Saucy Fish Co. launched a range that takes the fuss out of it. Hey Presto! A shoal of inspiring fish and sauce combinations.

thesaucyfishco.com

Photo credit: Addie Chinn

The Zetter Townhouse Clerkenwell

Like the private home of an eccentric ancestor, The Zetter Townhouse Clerkenwell is a magical, Alice in Wonderland meets Charles Dickens experience that delights at every turn.

Created by The Zetter Group, this 13-bedroom Georgian townhouse has reinterpreted the boutique hotel concept. Located on the historic St. John's Square, it features a sumptuous lounge replete with oddities and curios, where an apothecary-style bar dispenses exceptional cocktails. Meanwhile, bedrooms – from the whimsical to the majestic – offer a luxurious antidote to any revelry enjoyed in the lounge below. A new addition to the family – The Zetter Townhouse Marylebone – will open in August 2015.

thezettertownhouse.com

TONI&GUY

Celebrating more than 50 years of hair, fashion and heritage, TONI&GUY is renowned within the hair industry for innovation and bridging the gap between high fashion and hairdressing.

One of the most powerful hairdressing brands in the world, with more than 475 salons worldwide, TONI&GUY has helped to change the face of the industry on an international scale. Providing the ultimate link between fashion and hair, it is the Official Sponsor of London Fashion Week, the Scottish Fashion Awards and the British Fashion Awards. Its professional haircare range, label.m, is the Official Product of London Fashion Week, the first brand to receive this endorsement by the British Fashion Council.

toniandguy.com

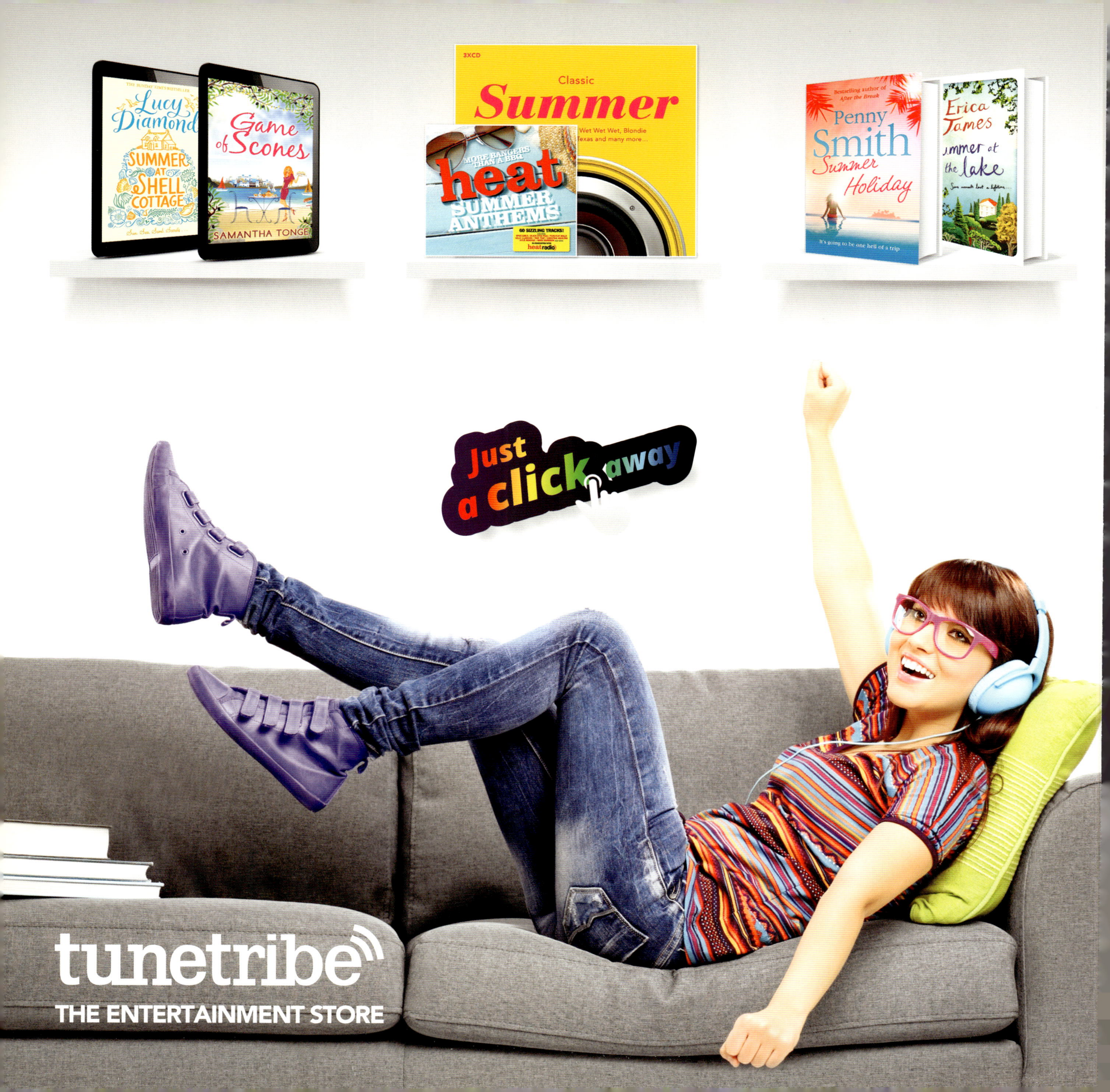

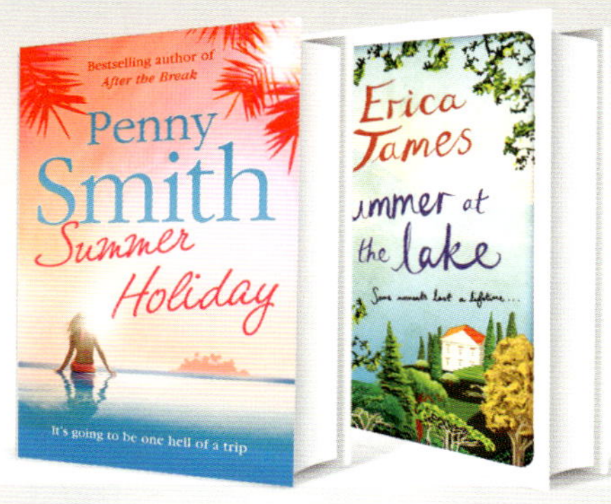

tunetribe
THE ENTERTAINMENT STORE

Tunetribe

Now much more than a music store, Tunetribe has evolved over the past year and added exciting new products for everyone's entertainment needs.

With a new landing page and an exciting new look to its product pages with enhanced functionality, Tunetribe is the ultimate digital entertainment store. In addition, through Tunetribe Digital, brands are able to utilise its industry expertise in music, books and digital development to create exciting programmes and affiliate deals. It provides a variety of services such as e-vouchers for all of its products and white label sites, if required. All just a click away.

tunetribe.com

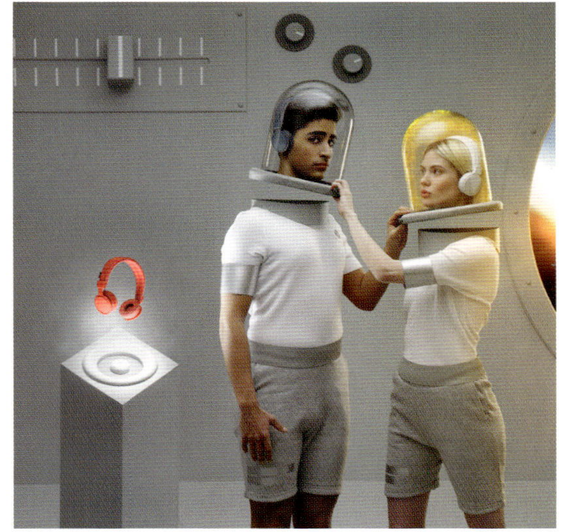

Urbanears

Based in Stockholm, Sweden, Urbanears supplies the perfect listening device for anyone with a pocket full of music and a wish to make the most of it.

Urbanears makes headphones that fit everyday life, with models designed to optimize sound and captivate self-aware customers by matching preferences in size, style, design, function and relation to music. Other companies may try to emulate the brand, but Urbanears is the original in colorful headphones. Urbanears is intended to be accessible to any person, regardless of who they are, rather than connecting the brand to a certain genre of music, fashion or subculture.

URBANEARS™

urbanears.com

Virgin Atlantic

A sense of adventure, friendly, intuitive service and customer-focused innovation make Virgin Atlantic the airline for people who want flying to be truly inspiring.

With its latest ad campaign, Virgin Atlantic urges travellers to grab life and 'let it fly' – a philosophy the brand itself has pursued from its inaugural flight in 1984 through to 2014's Flight Decks event, which saw the world's first live gig broadcast from 35,000 feet. Recent customer innovations include a California inspired Clubhouse lounge at LA airport and an incredible 787-9 Dreamliner with destination-timed mood lighting and a brighter, fresher on board environment for crew and customers.

virgin-atlantic.com

London Lounge

2015 Virgin Money London Marathon

Glasgow Lounge

Sex Pistols Credit Cards

Virgin Money

The Virgin brand has been shaking up various industries for more than 40 years. Now Virgin Money is on a quest to make banking better.

Small changes can add up to make a big difference. So Virgin Money never stops looking at how every bit of banking works. Gone are boring branches, replaced by inviting Stores and customer Lounges. Through its not-for-profit fundraising website, Virgin Money Giving, the bank uses its expertise to do some good in the world. And Virgin Money isn't afraid to do things other banks won't, like putting the Sex Pistols on its credit card. All with the aim of shaking up banking.

virginmoney.com

Zoffany

With a reputation for timeless yet innovative design, Zoffany provides luxurious fabrics, wallpapers, paint and upholstery, creating an elegant aesthetic in both contemporary and classic interiors.

Zoffany is a luxury interior furnishings brand with elegance and heritage at its core. Inspired by a unique archive, together with technical innovation, the dedicated Zoffany design team create beautifully crafted artwork that is translated into inspirational products of the highest quality. Zoffany's exquisite fabrics, wallpapers, paint and upholstery are selected by the world's interior designers for the creation of beautiful interiors.

ZOFFANY

zoffany.com

Expert Council 2015/16

Much more than merely a 'trend', coolness is a distinctive, elusive quality. It can be found in many things, but can never be forced. So how do we decide who makes the CoolBrands® cut? Our Expert Council – a hand-picked team of 36 style gurus, thought leaders, instigators and innovators – were challenged with separating the coolest from all the rest.

Chairman, CoolBrands®
Expert Council

Stephen Cheliotis
Chief Executive, The Centre
for Brand Analysis (TCBA)
@TCBA_London

A leading brand commentator and consultant, Stephen's work at TCBA includes brand evaluation and perception studies, strategic planning for brand owners and market analysis. Stephen also produces studies for agencies, speaks at conferences, comments on branding issues for the media and acts as an expert witness in brand disputes.

Alex Lawther
Actor

Amanda Wakeley OBE
Fashion Designer
@AmandaWakeley

Amelia Liana
Beauty & Fashion Vlogger
@AmeliaLiana_

With acclaimed performances across film, theatre, television and radio to his name, Alex is best known for playing a young Alan Turing in The Imitation Game. Winner of the Young British Performer of the Year at the London Critics' Circle Film Awards in 2014, Alex was also nominated for Best British Newcomer at the BFI London Film Festival.

Amanda launched her signature line and opened a small studio boutique in the heart of London in 1990. Since 2009, she has built her brand and business with the lifestyle approach she had always envisioned and can now count Beyoncé, Helen Mirren and Angelina Jolie as fans. Amanda has won three British Fashion Awards and has co-chaired the committee for Fashion Targets Breast Cancer since 1996.

Style and beauty influencer Amelia stormed onto the YouTube scene in 2013 with her channel and blog, amelialiana, and has quickly developed a cherished relationship with her growing audience. Her relaxed style and charm have made her a trusted confidante to her followers, enabling her to deliver invaluable advice and guidance on more delicate topics beyond traditional beauty and fashion.

Billie JD Porter
Journalist & Film Maker
@billiejdporter

Caroline Rush CBE
CEO, British Fashion Council
@rushcaroline

Charlotte Moore
Editor, InStyle
@Charl_InStyle

The 22-year old London girl, Billie, has already amassed an impressive career online, in print and on television. She has written for titles such as Vice, Dazed & Confused, Wonderland as well as NME and made documentaries for the BBC and Channel 4. Billie has also posed for Louis Vuitton and Levi's and is known for her unique sense of style.

CEO since 2009, Caroline has strengthened London Fashion Week and support for British design talent, expanded the LONDON show ROOMS and Style Suites, taking British designers to new global markets. She launched Britain Creates, part of the Fashion 2012 platform, to celebrate the Olympic and Paralympic Games and the Cultural Olympiad, and London Collections: Men, one of the four global leading showcases for designer menswear.

With more than 15 years' experience in fashion, celebrity and features journalism and positions held at Marie Claire, Marie Claire Runway, ELLE and InStyle, Charlotte has been Editor of InStyle since February 2014. In summer 2014 she oversaw a redesign of the magazine and the website.

'Cool is being rebellious while being able to put something good back into the world.' Alex Lawther

Charlotte Riley
Actress

David Harewood MBE
Actor
@DavidHarewood

Ella Eyre
Singer-Songwriter
@EllaEyre

After playing Sarah Hurst in Easy Virtue, Charlotte went on to star as Catherine Earnshaw in ITV's adaptation of Wuthering Heights. Recent projects include the film Heart of the Sea, and starring alongside Tom Cruise in Edge of Tomorrow. Charlotte has also joined the cast of BBC's Peaky Blinders and Jonathan Strange & Mr Norrell.

A RADA graduate, David has received huge critical acclaim for his work in theatre, cinema and television. He played Captain Poison in the Oscar-nominated Blood Diamond and starred in hit US drama Homeland. In 2015 David has appeared in Spooks: The Greater Good with Peter Firth and Jennifer Ehle, Tulip Fever alongside Judi Dench, as well as featuring in Grimsby with Sacha Baron Cohen and Mark Strong.

With a clutch of BRIT and MOBO awards to her name, the past year has seen Ella release two singles, write and feature on DJ Fresh's Gravity and co-write the number one single, Changing, for Sigma and Paloma Faith. In 2015 she released her single, Together, debut album, Feline, and was announced as the new face of Emporio Armani Diamonds.

Jaime Winstone
Actress
@JWinstone

With credits spanning TV, film and theatre, Jaime is best known for her roles in Kidulthood, Bullet Boy and Made in Dagenham. She starred in BAFTA-nominated drama Dead Set in 2008, won an RTS Award for Best Actress in 2010 and is soon to be seen in Sky's After Hours.

Jamal Edwards MBE
Entrepreneur & Founder, SB.TV
@jamaledwards

Described as 'one of Britain's hottest young entrepreneurs' by the Evening Standard, Jamal founded SB.TV aged 15. With over 300 million YouTube views, SB.TV has featured interviews with guests ranging from Richard Branson to Prince Charles. His business ebook, Self Belief: The Vision, was a bestseller and he has curated stages at Bestival and Wireless. Jamal received an MBE for services to music in 2014.

James-lee Duffy
Creative Director, A Little Bird & Founder, Pavement Licker
@jamesleeduffy

James has worked on brands such as BACARDÍ, LEGO and Nintendo to name a few. His illustration work has shown internationally and he has been commissioned by the likes of Panasonic, Dr Martens and Nike. His 'zine, Pavement Licker, is found in cities across the world and has featured contributions from such names as Shepard Fairey and Banksy.

Jonathan Bailey
Actor
@JonnyBailey

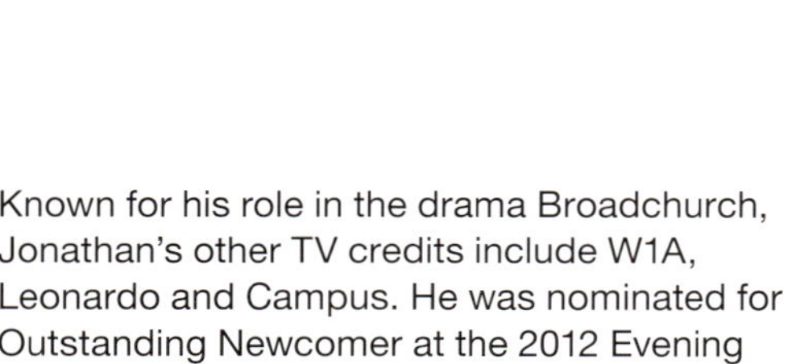

Known for his role in the drama Broadchurch, Jonathan's other TV credits include W1A, Leonardo and Campus. He was nominated for Outstanding Newcomer at the 2012 Evening Standard Awards and recently played Cassio in Othello at the National Theatre. Film credits include Testament of Youth and What We Did on Our Holiday.

Julien Macdonald OBE
Fashion Designer
@JulienMacdonald

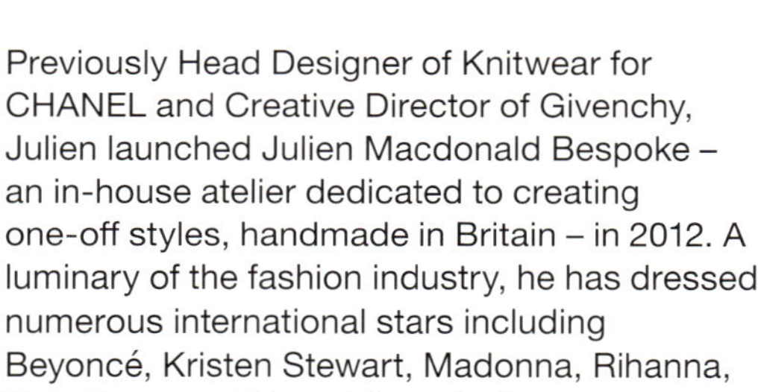

Previously Head Designer of Knitwear for CHANEL and Creative Director of Givenchy, Julien launched Julien Macdonald Bespoke – an in-house atelier dedicated to creating one-off styles, handmade in Britain – in 2012. A luminary of the fashion industry, he has dressed numerous international stars including Beyoncé, Kristen Stewart, Madonna, Rihanna, Katy Perry and Naomi Campbell.

Justin Wilkes
DJ, Kisstory/Kiss FM UK
@justinwilkes

One of the UK's most respected music radio presenters, Justin hosts Kisstory every weekday morning and Kiss FM UK's Hang Out show every weekday afternoon. A renowned club DJ, he is famed for his sets at major product launches and for voicing international advertising campaigns. Justin also has his own Luxury Home Technology brand, and is at the cutting-edge of cool.

Kate Halfpenny
Fashion Designer & Stylist
@Halfpennylondon

Kelly Hoppen MBE
**Designer, Author
& Entrepreneur**
@IMKellyHoppen

Labrinth
Singer-Songwriter
@Labrinthda1st

Celebrity stylist and fashion designer, Kate is famed for her bespoke creations worn by amazing women such as Rihanna, Erin O'Connor and Kate Moss. She creates costumes for brands such as Hugo Boss, PlayStation and L'Oréal. Her first bridal boutique opened in Bloomsbury in 2013 with her entirely British made collection. Halfpenny London is no longer an industry secret.

A globally renowned designer, Kelly has one of the most celebrated careers in the creative industry. The recipient of numerous awards including an MBE for services to interior design, she is ambassador for the Prince's Trust and the Government's GREAT Campaign. Her studio currently runs over 50 projects and she recently launched an online store, kellyhoppen.com.

Having re-imagined the perimeters of pop music's soundscape, Labrinth now has more than five million sales to his name since releasing Let the Sun Shine in 2010. His debut album, Electronic Earth, hit number two in the charts and he's picked up an Ivor Novello, a MOBO award and a BRIT nomination. His second album, Take me to the Truth, was released in 2015.

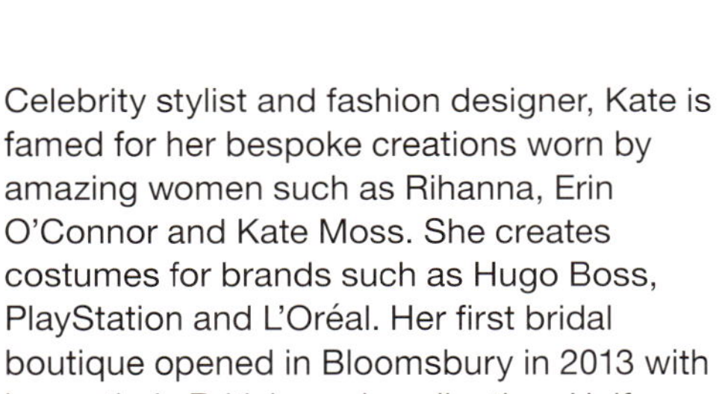

'2015 is the year for our social stars. Celebrities famous-for-being-famous will move aside for vloggers and YouTube stars who have caught the attention of millions of new users.' Natasha McNamara

Laura Jackson
TV Presenter
@IamLauraJackson

Liz Matthews
Publicist
@lizmatthewspr

Lucy Siegle
Journalist & Presenter
@lucysiegle

Having started her career on T4's music show Freshly Squeezed, Laura most recently hosted Take Me Out - The Gossip alongside Mark Wright, and is one of TV's brightest rising stars. She has spent two seasons as a backstage reporter at London Fashion Week, and has a host of fashion and music presenting jobs and interviews under her belt.

An entertainment publicist with more than a decade of experience, Liz's client list includes Alexa Chung, Laura Bailey, Sophie Dahl and Karen Elson. LMPR brands launched in 2013 and accounts include Loquet London, Leighton Denny and Caramel Baby & Child.

Ethical agony aunt for the Observer and Guardian, Lucy is author of To Die For: Is Fashion Wearing Out the World? She has given sell out talks for TEDx and is known to millions as a presenter on The One Show. A trustee of Forum for the Future, she founded the Green Carpet Challenge with Livia Firth and executive produced the documentary The True Cost (of fashion).

'Whether it's a product, brand or even an industry, to revolutionise something is what cool means to me in 2015.'
Melissa Odabash

Mark Krendel
Managing Director, 8lbs
@8lbsUK

Melissa Odabash
Fashion Designer
@melissaodabash

Michelle Ogundehin
Editor-in-Chief, ELLE Decoration UK
@MOgundehin

Mark has more than a decade's experience structuring commercial deals in the entertainment industry. Having helped establish the digital and commercial divisions at Universal Music, he founded entertainment partnerships specialist, 8lbs, in 2012. Mark's growing team has delivered campaigns for the likes of boohoo, HSBC and Sony Xperia and increasingly invest in emerging businesses and platforms.

Launched in 1999, Melissa's first swimwear collection swiftly came to epitomize the glamour of a luxury lifestyle brand. Her partnerships include working with Julien Macdonald for resort wear collection Odabash & Macdonald and Gwyneth Paltrow for her website, GOOP. Melissa has also worked with the Elton John AIDS Foundation, and breast cancer charity Future Dreams on her debut mastectomy swimwear collection.

An internationally respected authority on style and design, Michelle's 10-year tenure at ELLE Decoration has seen the magazine's circulation rise to the highest in its 25-year history. She has contributed to publications including Numéro, ID Magazine, Hochparterre, The Face, Arena and The Observer, and has held positions as Interiors Editor of Esquire and Nova magazine. She has also been a Trustee of the V&A since 2008.

Millie Kendall MBE

@MillieKendall

Alongside Anna-Marie Solowij, Millie is Co-Founder of BeautyMART, a disruptive retail concept for beauty at Harvey Nichols, Shoreditch and Topshop as well as online at thisisbeautymart.com. Millie has been instrumental in the success of many cult beauty brands, from Shu Uemura and Aveda to Ruby & Millie and Concoction Haircare.

Natasha McNamara

@shadyalabama

Working across lifestyle and fashion websites since 2006, Natasha is Digital Editor of glamour.com, where she oversees the creative direction of the fashion, beauty and celebrity editorial. Natasha won Launch of the Year 2012 for the launch of easyliving.co.uk – now houseandgardenmagazine.co.uk – at the British Society of Magazine Editors Award.

Patrick Goss

@patrickgoss

Patrick Goss is the Global Editor-in-Chief of TechRadar, one of the world's biggest consumer technology sites. He spent the early part of his career with SkySports.com and often suggests that this makes him the only journalist to have covered both a World Cup final and an iPhone queue.

Perou
Master Fashion &
Portrait Photographer
@mrperou

Perou specialises in fashion, editorial and portrait photography and is one of the most iconic and inspirational figures in the industry. Creator of the popular E4 TV show Dirty Sexy Things his clientele includes the likes of Vogue, Q Magazine and Levi's, as well as individuals such as 50 Cent, Samuel L. Jackson, Jay Z, Daft Punk, David Beckham and Justin Timberlake.

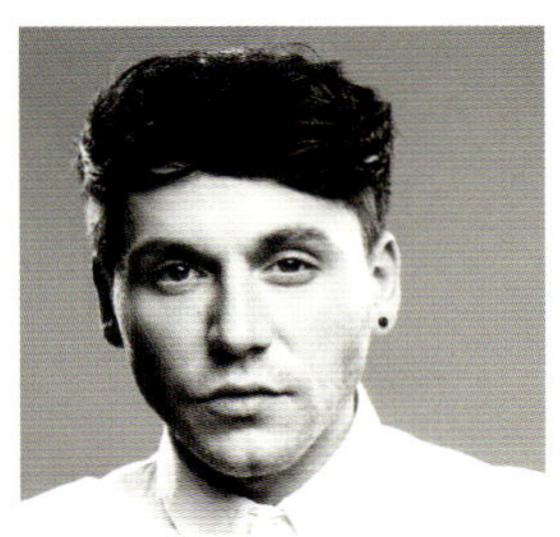

Phil Clifton
XFM DJ & Presenter
@philclifton

A Sony-nominated radio presenter, Phil currently DJ's for XFM. He also works as a TV presenter, having hosted shows for MTV, Freshly Squeezed, the BRIT Awards 2012 and Channel 5. He has performed sets at major events including the NME Awards and London Fashion Week, and was recently announced as the new host of the Friday Night Request Show across the XFM Network.

Ruby Hammer MBE
Make-Up Artist
@RubyMakeup

Having had a pioneering influence on the fashion and beauty industries for more than 25 years, Ruby is one of the most respected makeup artists in the world. She has created and been involved with a whole host of cool brands, from Aveda and TweezerMan to Ruby & Millie, and has recently launched her digital platform, rubyhammer.com.

'Cool is easy like lemon squeezy – apparently effortless, not contrived or learnt. Cool can't be media trained or brainstormed, you just HAVE it... or you don't.' Perou

Sadie Frost
Actress, Producer
& Fashion Designer
@Sadieliza

Sadie co-founded Frostfrench in 1999. It now has two highly successful brands within designers at Debenhams – Floozie and Iris & Edie – which encompass swimwear, lingerie and handbags. Sadie also has a production company, Blonde to Black Pictures, which has completed two feature films, Buttercup Bill and Set the Thames on Fire, as well as award-winning shorts such as Dotty.

Sam Hall (Goldierocks)
International DJ &
Broadcaster
@Goldierocks

Host of a weekly global radio show, The Selector, international DJ and broadcaster Sam Hall (Goldierocks) can be heard in over 40 countries worldwide with an audience of over 4.3 million weekly listeners. She routinely performs on the main stages of the world's most popular festivals, as well as travelling the world for philanthropic work with a range of charities.

Susan Riley
Deputy Editor,
Stylist Magazine
@Susestylist

Having spent more than a decade in the women's and lifestyle publishing sectors, Susan has been Deputy Editor – and twice Acting Editor – of multi-award winning Stylist magazine since its launch in 2009. As part of Shortlist Media Limited's senior editorial team, she's also worked on the development of Stylist France and digital fashion glossy, Never Underdressed.

'Cool in 2015 is being experience-rich. Forget what you've got; it's all about where you've been, things you've seen and what you're planning next.' Susan Riley

Tim Beaumont
Founder, Beaumont Communications
@beaumontlondon

Tim founded Beaumont Communications in 2011 and has worked in the entertainment industry for over 10 years. The agency boasts exciting artists across film, television, music, food and fashion with actors, directors, chefs, DJs, presenters comedians and YouTubers on the roster including Maxine Peake, Vicky McClure, Jim Chapman, Millie Mackintosh, Rob da Bank and Gizzi Erskine.

Will Best
TV Presenter & Music Entrepreneur
@iamwillbest

Previously part of the T4 family, Will's presenting career has seen him go on to present for Simon Cowell's You Generation, 4Music, New Look Online and he also has an upcoming show on BBC3. With a contagious passion for all things music, Will is also one of the Founders of electronic music sharing site audiosplitter.fm.

Qualifying CoolBrands® 2015/16

& Other Stories
Abel & Cole
ABSOLUT VODKA
Ace Hotel
ACHICA
Acne Studios
Acqua di Parma
Acqua Panna
Activision Blizzard
adidas
Aēsop
Affordable Art Fair
AGA
Agent Provocateur
Airbnb
Albion
Alessi
Alex Monroe
Alexander McQueen
Alexander Wang
Alexandra Palace
Alienware
AllSaints
Alternative Flooring
Amazon Prime
American Apparel
Angostura
Anolon
Anya Hindmarch
Apple
Appleton Estate
Aquazzura
Argent and Sable
Aromatherapy
   Associates
Artisan du Chocolat
Asahi
ASICS
ASOS
Aspall Cyder
Aston Martin
Atsuko Kudo
Audi
Aurelia Probiotic
   Skincare
Aveda
B&B Italia
Badoit
Balfour
Balthazar

Bang & Olufsen
Barbican
bareMinerals
Barry's Bootcamp
BBC
BBC iPlayer
BEAR
Bea's of Bloomsbury
Beats by Dr. Dre
Bed Head
BELAZU
Belkin
Belu Water
Belvedere Vodka
Ben & Jerry's
Benefit
Bentley
Berners Tavern
Berry Bros. & Rudd
Bert & May
Bestival
Bicester Village
Big Tom
Biona
Bisque
black + blum
Black Cow
Black Dragon
Black Eyewear
Black Vanilla
Blaupunkt
blk.
BLOOM
BLOOM Gin
BMW
Bobbi Brown
Bocca di Lupo
BoConcept
BODIE and FOU
Bodum
Boffi
Bollinger
Bombay Sapphire
Booja-Booja
BOOM Cycle
Bootcamp Pilates
Borough Market
Bose
Bottega Veneta
Bounce Energy Balls

Bowers & Wilkins
Boxerchips
BOXPARK
BrewDog
British Airways
Brocks Chocs
Brompton
Brooklyn Brewery
BULLDOG
bulthaup
Bumble and bumble
Burberry
Burger & Lobster
Burts Potato Chips
Buster & Punch
Butler's Gin
Byredo
C.P. Hart
Cambridge Audio
Cambridge Satchel
   Company
Camden Town
   Brewery
Canon
Capital FM
Caravan
Carnaby
Carousel Lights
Casamigos Tequila
Cawston Press
Cereal Killer Cafe
Champagne Perrier-
   Jouët
CHANEL
Channel 4
Chapel Down
Charbonnel et Walker
Charlotte Olympia
Charlotte Tilbury
Chase
Chiltern Firehouse
Chivas Regal
Chocolate Tree
Christian Louboutin
Christopher Kane
Church's
Ciaté
Cire Trudon
Citymapper
Clarins

Clipper
CND
Coco de Mer
Cole & Mason
Comedy Central
COMME des
   GARÇONS
Conscious Chocolate
Converse All Stars
Cornish Orchards
COS
Courvoisier
Covent Garden
Cream & Country
Creed
Crème de la Mer
Crussh
Crystal Head Vodka
Cuckoo
Cutter & Squidge
Damaris
Darling Spuds
Dave
Daylesford
Deezer
De'Longhi
Dermalogica
Designed in Colour
Designers Guild
Destinology
Dinner by Heston
   Blumenthal
Dior
diptyque
Discovery Channel
Dishoom
Doble & Bignall
Dom Pérignon
Dominic Jones
Doom Bar
Dover Street Market
DQ Vodka
Dr. Hauschka
Dr. Martens
Dualit
Ducati
Duck & Waffle
EA
East London Liquor
   Company

Eden Project
Edinburgh International
   Festival
Elephant Gin
Elite London
Ella's Kitchen
EMI
essie
Estrella Damm
Etsy
EVE LOM
evian
Eyeko
Fabletics
Facebook
FALKE
Farfetch
Farrow & Ball
Feel Good Drinks
Fentimans
Ferrari
Fever-Tree
FEW Spirits
Fibre Flare
Fiddler's Lancashire
   Crisps
Field Day
Fired Earth
Firefly
Firmdale Hotels
first direct
Fisher & Paykel
Fitbit
Fitbug
Five Guys
Flickr
Flos
Forza
Foyles
Frame
Fred & Ginger
Freya
Frieze Art Fair
Fritz Hansen
Frostfrench
Gaggenau
Gaggia
GAIL'S
GameStick
Garmin

Gaucho
ghd
Gilpin's Gin
Glastonbury
Google
GoPro
Gousto
Graham & Brown
graze.com
Green & Black's
   Organic
Green Man Festival
Gressingham Duck
Grey Goose
Grove Organic Fruit Co
Gü
Guinness
GYMBOX
Häagen-Dazs
Haig Club
Ham Yard Hotel
Hampstead Tea
Harley-Davidson
Harrogate Spring
   Water
Harry Brompton's
   London Ice Tea
Harvey Nichols
Hasselblad
Hawksmoor
HAY
Hayman's
Heal's
Heartcore
Hectares
HelloFresh
Hendrick's Gin
Hennessy
Henney's
Hernö Gin
Hershesons
hey jo
HILLIER
HIP Hotels
Hive
Hix
Hogan's Cider
Home House
Honest Burgers
Hotel Café Royal

Hotel Chocolat
House Envy
House of Hackney
Houzz
HoxtonHotels
HTC
Hublot
Hummus Bros
Hunter
Hyperdub
Ice Cream Union
ila
IMG Models
Independent
innocent
Instagram
Isle of Wight Festival
itsu
ITV
Jack Daniel's
Jaguar
Jameson
Jamie Oliver (Products)
Jawbone
Jax Coco
Jelly Belly
Jimmy Choo
Jimmy's Iced Coffee
JO LOVES
Jo Malone
Joe & Seph's
John Frieda
John Lewis
Johnnie Walker
Jose Cuervo
Joseph Joseph
Jude's
Juniper Green Organic
   Gin
Kawasaki
KEF
Kérastase
Ketel One Vodka
KETTLE Chips
Kiehl's
Kindle
Kirk & Kirk
KitchenAid
Konami
Konditor & Cook

Konik's Tail
Kopparberg
Korres
Krispy Kreme
Kriss Soonik
Krug
KRUPS
Kurobuta
La Perla
Laboratory Perfumes
Lamborghini
Langley's No.8
Lanvin
Laphroaig
Lara Bohinc
L'Artisan Parfumeur
Last.fm
Latitude
Laura Mercier
Laurent-Perrier
Lavazza
Le Chameau
Le Creuset
Leatherman
Leica
Leighton Denny
Lékué
Lenovo
Leon
Levi's
LG
Liberty
LIBRARY
Lick
Ligne Roset
Lilou et Loïc
Lime Wood
Linda Farrow
Lindt
Linn
Little Greene
Little Miracles
Liverpool ONE
Loaf.com
L'OCCITANE
Loewe
Lomography
London Art Fair
London Designer
    Outlet
London Fields Brewery
Louis Roederer
Løv Organic
Lovebox
LoveRaw
LSA International
LUMIX
Luscombe
LUXE City Guides
M.A.C
Mackie's of Scotland
Made.com
Magimix
Magners
Maison Assouline

Maker's Mark
Manolo Blahnik
Marmite
Marou, Faiseurs de
    Chocolat
Martin Miller's Gin
Maserati
Mast Brothers
MATCHESFASHION.COM
McLaren Automotive
Meantime
MEATliquor
Megelli
Mercedes-Benz
Mercier Champagne
Metcalfe's skinny
Methven
Miele
MiLK
MINI
Minotti
Minx Nails
Misfit
Miu Miu
Models 1
Moët & Chandon
Moleskine
Mondrian London
    at Sea Containers
Monica Vinader
Monkey 47
Monkey Shoulder
Monmouth
mophie
Morgan
Moroccanoil
Moto Guzzi
Mövenpick Ice Cream
Mr & Mrs Smith
Mr Organic
MR PORTER
Mr. Hare
MTV
Mulberry
Mungo & Maud
Murdock London
MUVI
MV Agusta
Myla
Nails inc
Nakd
Naked Wines
NARS
National Anthem
Neal's Yard Remedies
NEFF
Neom Organics
Nespresso
Nest
Nest.co.uk
NET-A-PORTER.COM
Netflix
nevs
New Balance
Nicolas Kirkwood

Nike
Nike+ FuelBand
Nikon
Nintendo
No.3 London Dry Gin
No1 Lounges
Norton Motorcycles
Nota Bene
notonthehighstreet.com
NOW TV
Nutribullet
Nyetimber
O2 Academy
Oculus Rift
Old Jamaica Ginger
    Beer
Old Mout Cider
Oliver Goldsmith
Oliver Peoples
Olivia von Halle
Olympus
onefinestay
Only Fingers + Toes
OPI
Orchard Pig
Oribe
ORLY
Ortigia
Osborne & Little
Ottolenghi
Oxford Covered
    Market
Parklife
Parrot Zik
Pashley
Pastino's
Patagonia
Patrón Tequila
Paul
Pebble
Penhaligon's
Pentax
Percy & Reed
Peroni Nastro Azzurro
Perrier
Perry Court Farm
Persol
Peyton and Byrne
Philip Kingsley
Phyto
Piaggio
Pimm's
Pinkberry
Pinterest
Planet Organic
PlayStation
Plenish
pod
Poet Audio
Poggenpohl
Polar
Polaroid
Police
Pollen Street Social
Polpo

popchips
Porsche
Portobello Road
    Market
Prada
Premier Model
    Management
Prestat
Pret A Manger
PROPERCORN
Psycle
Pukka
Puma
Qobuz
Quintessentially Group
Rare Tea Company
Raw Health
Ray-Ban
Razer
Rdio
REAL Crisps
Real Techniques
reddit
Reebok
Rekorderlig
Rémy Martin
REN
Restaurant Nathan
    Outlaw
Riedel
Rigby & Peller
Righteous
Riverford
Robert Welch
Roberts Radio
Rockett St George
Rockstar Games
Rococo Chocolates
Rodial
Rolex
Rolls-Royce
Ron Zacapa
Rosewood London
Royal Albert Hall
Royal Dragon Vodka
Royal Enfield
Ruark Audio
Ruinart
Runtastic
Rupert Sanderson
Russian Standard
    Vodka
S.Pellegrino
Sage Gateshead
Sailor Jerry
Salty Dog
Samsung
San Miguel
Sandford Orchards
Sarah Chapman
Sauza Tequila
SB.TV
Scarlett & Mustard
SCP
Seabrook Crisps

Secret Garden Party
SEGA
Select Model
    Management
Selfridges
Sennheiser
Seven Dials
Shakespeare's Globe
Shangri-La Hotel at
    The Shard
Sharpham Park
Shazam
Shiseido
Shu Uemura
Shuffler
Sipsmith
Sisley
SkinCeuticals
Skinny Champagne
Skinny Cow
Sky Atlantic
Sky Garden at 20
    Fenchurch Street
Skype
Smeg
Smooze
Snapchat
Snog
Snoozebox
Soho House & Co
Sonos
Sony
Sony Music
Sophia Webster
SoundCloud
Soundway Records
Southbank Centre
Space NK
Speedflex
Speyside Glenlivet
Spitalfields
Spotify
Spotted by Locals
St David's
St. Peter's Brewery
Stella McCartney
Stephen Webster
Sticks'n'Sushi
Stokes Sauces
Storm
SUSHISAMBA
Suzuki
Swoon Editions
tado°
TAG Heuer
Taittinger
Tangle Teezer
Tanqueray
TAU Spring Water
Taylors of Harrogate
teapigs
Tempo Pilates
TenPilates
Terry de Havilland
Tesla

The Artisan Kitchen
The Arts Club
The Beaumont
The Berry Company
The Botanist
The Breakfast Club
The Clove Club
The Club at the Ivy
The Connaught
The Cornish Crisp
    Company
The Dormen Food
    Company
The Duppy Share
The Fat Duck
The Five Points
    Brewing Company
The French Bedroom
    Company
The Garrick Club
The Gifted Few
The Glenlivet
The Hand and Flowers
The Hospital Club
The House of
    St Barnabas
The Kernel Brewery
The Kooples
The Kraken
The London Distillery
    Company
The London EDITION
The London Tea
    Company
The Macallan
The New Craftsmen
The North Face
The O2
The Original Candy
    Company
THE OUTNET
The Palomar
The Pig
The Place
The Rug Company
The Saucy Fish Co.
The Third Space
The White Company
The Wild Peanut
The Zetter Townhouse
Thirsty Planet
Thomas J Fudge's
Three Olives
Tiffany & Co.
Tiger Beer
Tom Daxon
Tom Dixon
TOM FORD
TONI&GUY
Topshop
Toshiba
Tossed
Tough Mudder
Trinity Leeds
Triumph

triyoga
Tumblr
Tunetribe
Twinings
Twitter
Ty Nant
Typing Room
Tyrrells
Uber
Ubisoft
Universal Music Group
Urban Decay
Urban Fruit
Urbanears
Valrhona
VALT
Vans
Vespa
Veuve Clicquot
VEVO
Victoria's Secret
Victory Motorcycles
Villeroy & Boch
Vimeo
Vine
Virgin Atlantic
Virgin Money
Vita Coco
Vita Liberata
Vitamix
Vitra
Vivienne Westwood
Vivitek
VOSS
WAH Nails
Wahoo Fitness
Warner Music
we are tea
Westfield
Westons Cider
Whistles
Whole Foods Market
Wilderness
William Morris
    Endeavor
Withings
Wolford
Wyborowa
Xbox
XFM
Yamaha
yoomoo
Yorkshire Crisps
Yorkshire Provender
Yorvale
YouTube
Zanzan
Zapp
Zara
ZenZen
Zipcar
Zoffany